TO THE PLACE OF SHELLS

By the same Author

*

A GUARD WITHIN

TO THE
PLACE OF SHELLS

Sarah Ferguson

1975
CHATTO & WINDUS
LONDON

Published by
Chatto & Windus Ltd.
42 William IV Street
London WC2N 4DF

*

Clarke, Irwin & Co. Ltd.
Toronto

ISBN 0 7011 2101 7

Printed in Great Britain by
Ebenezer Baylis & Son, Ltd.
The Trinity Press, Worcester, and London

ACKNOWLEDGMENT

The poem by T. S. Eliot, *Song :* '*The moonflower opens to the moth*', is reprinted by kind permission of Faber & Faber Ltd.

PART 1

And bugles calling for them from sad shires.
                              Wilfred Owen

Maybrook is a small village in Northamptonshire. It has an Early English church with a broach spire and Norman arches, and it has a seventeenth-century house known as Maybrook Hall. It lies in the north of the county, in a land where church spires rise out of the fields as though they had grown there, like the ancient elms which populate this place, or the willows which stand in the waters of the River Nene. All around the grey spires ascend above the villages, foretelling the glory of Peterborough – Warmington, Hemington, Lutton and Glapthorn, and then there is Maybrook.

Maybrook Hall: a grey Jacobean house with a balustraded terrace. The flight of steps leads to the courtyard below. The high iron gates with their intricate pattern open into the road. The stone shepherd with his shepherdess who stand on the gate pillars, beckon lovingly to each other. Through the iron pattern of the gates only the façade of the house is seen. Not an inch is allowed for a view of the garden or the stable yard where my mother grew and played and lived and loved so intensely. It was here that my sister and I were brought to be cared for by our grandparents when my mother died of a heart disease on her birthday at the age of thirty-three. I was three and my sister seven. In the dark billiard room my grandmother sat on the leather settee to tell us of our mother's death. My sister cried but I pretended not to hear. I continued to play with my doll, fussing over it busily, but in my heart I knew that catastrophe had struck. The low hanging

lights over the billiard table gave no light. My grandmother twisted the sapphire rings on her fingers and said
no more.

On the day of my mother's funeral we were sent with
our Nan to spend the day with a family named Peacock.
My sister Margaret's friend was Ingrid, a child the same
age as herself. My companion was a baby girl in a white
muslin cot covered in frills. I rustled the spotted muslin
with my hand and peered in at the sleeping baby. I wanted
to pick her up and kill her. A mounting anger grew within
me, but all I could do was to stare and stare at this perfect
sleeping infant. It was supposed to be a treat for us to visit
the Peacocks for the day, but I knew we were being sent
away from our mother while they buried her in the churchyard. That night, safely back in my cot, I wanted to go
and dig her up. Dig her out of the grave where I only
imagined they had laid her. I had told myself that she
would return; that she had gone away to a distant
country and I would one day see her again, see her pale
fair hair and skin, see her lying in bed in the mornings
offering me a small roundabout to play with, which I
found so uninteresting I always wanted to smash it.

*   *   *

The absence of my mother appeared to make very little
difference to us. Our father was sent away to the war and
we continued to live happily at Maybrook with our grandparents. My grandfather was crippled with gout and rode
in an electric chair, but was a jovial retired brigadier-
general with a large white moustache who sang songs of
the First World War when we came down for lunch to the
dining-room on Sundays. I see the oak-panelled room with

the rows of pewter plates hanging round the walls, the long shining table scattered with silver objects and Albert the footman handing me a plate of roast beef before the rationing began and before he too was sent away to the war. My grandmother rapped her rings on the table if we did not sit up straight and my grandfather thumped his swollen gouty hands and sang: 'Dear Old Brown, upside down, with his feet sticking up in the air.'

The nursery was our refuge. Nan and our mother's Nan, Miss Offler, presided. Miss Offler was a small wiry woman of a great age, upright and full of energy, who clicked her teeth as she spoke. She always took a cold bath at six o'clock in the morning and acted as lady's-maid to our grandmother. She preserved the ostrich-feather fans which had been used at presentation parties and balls, and also the satin and lace page-boy costumes with their round broad-brimmed felt hats worn by our uncles. She wrapped them in tissue-paper and laid lavender bags beside them and stored them away in the tall cupboard in the nursery. The nursery was a pale green colour, which was rather faded. The pictures on the walls were of cherubs trailing garlands behind them as they floated through azure skies. There were also pictures of old hunting scenes. The horses had outstretched necks and large eyes and looked as though they were straining every muscle in their wooden-looking bodies. There was not much furniture in the nursery. There was an enormous sofa covered in a dirty-coloured flowery chintz, a table with a green and white checked cloth, a white toy cupboard with a musty smell, and a carved oak chest full of old-fashioned children's books. The largest thing in the nursery was the rocking-horse. It rocked on a wooden stand and had basket-chairs at each end. The horse's ears were chipped and its mane was very greasy. In the red leather saddle there was a hole where the pommel should have been. You could push things down through the hole so that they fell into the hollow body of the horse. Once they fell you could never get them back. If we rocked the horse too hard its stand thumped on the green linoleum floor and our grandfather rapped on the ceiling of his study, where he dealt with local affairs.

At night, after we had been put to bed, our grandmother would come to see us, dressed for dinner in her long velvet dress, her pearls and her white hair shining in the semi-darkness of the night-light, a faint aroma of lavender-water drifting in the air.

*   *   *

It was war. 1941. Nan told us the German soldiers did the 'goose-step'. What was the goose-step? I played the *Marche Lorraine* on the H.M.V. gramophone in the nursery and strutted up and down, dressed in my Guardsman's uniform.

It was a cold and wet winter's day. Nan took me for a walk in my push-chair. Not that she wanted to go but because it was her duty. 'Just up to the gypsy lane and back,' she said. Why was Nan so frightened that day? We knew that everyone was frightened. Why did we dig a deep hole in the flower-bed except to hide from the Germans? We did not know what invasion meant, but they said the Germans were coming. We walked through the stable yard where the rows of loose boxes which had once been full of hunters now stood empty. We walked through the back gate and out into the road. We took Sally, the black and white terrier, with us. I held her lead tightly in my hand. Nan walked too fast for Sally which she did not normally do. Nan's feet went click, click, click;

they pointed at ten to two in her lace-up shoes. I was cold even though I wore leggings and my green tweed coat and round felt hat. The wind blew. It whined and screamed in the telegraph wires along the road. The gigantic elms and the hedges were bare; the ditches were filled with water. The fields were ploughed in deep furrows, the tops covered in a crust of thawing frost. All the green fields were ploughed in order to provide enough corn for bread for the coming year.

We met Mrs. Smith on the road. The old, old woman who daily pushed her wicker cart full of newspapers for the village. Mrs. Smith never washed and her cottage was so dirty that no one ever visited her. But she was friendly with everyone and Nan stopped to talk to her, keeping her distance less than usual. They spoke in whispers but I overheard what they were saying. I now knew that a German parachutist had landed somewhere nearby. Nan walked faster and faster towards our goal. She was deter-mined to reach it but I sensed in her a frantic fear of the known and yet the unknown. I was frightened too. More frightened than ever in my life. I pulled my felt hat down over my nose; I shut my eyes tightly. The wind continued to moan and scream through the telegraph wires. Was there a German stumbling over the plough towards us with his giant white parachute billowing like a vast mush-room behind him? We would see him through the hedges and he could not hide behind the trees. Was he crouching in the red barn beside the cross-road where they had taken the signposts down? What would we do if we met him? He surely would shoot Nan and bury Sally and me under the ground alive. Nan did not talk or tell me stories as she usually did. I wished that the wind would stop screaming. He would come, he would come, the German. We reached the barricades of sandbags at the entrance to the village. If Nan could lift me over them they would not stop the

German or the tanks they spoke of. I clung to Nan but she pursed her mouth and walked on even faster until we reached the gates of the house.

That evening I put to bed in layers of cotton wool my rows of lead soldiers given me by my father. Nan listened to Lord Haw-Haw on the wireless. Who was Lord Haw-Haw? His name sounded important but funny also, but I knew that he was not funny. He was evil. The wireless was very large and made of wood with a soft material in front supported by criss-cross slats. 'Mr Churchill is going to speak,' said Nan. Nan, my sister Margaret and I sat in a row. I listened to the severity and seriousness of his voice which rose and sank with power. When his message was over we all stood to attention as we had been taught to do when the National Anthem was played. Then we had supper of soup cooked by Mrs. Underwood which we drank out of little brown pots. Nan curled my red hair in pieces of paper; little knots all over which rustled when I shook my head. Was it safe in the nursery beside the fire? It felt so. 'Do not let the German come,' I said. Nan shook her head and Nan Offler sucked her teeth in disapproval. They did not speak. And I thought of the German outside in the howling wind. Where was he that night? Was he hiding in the cold as afraid as myself? He had been sent away from his country perhaps never to return. I looked that night under the big carved oak bed in the night nursery which now Nan and I shared, to make certain that the German was not there.

*   *   *

In the vastness of my grandparents' garden there was a manor-house lived in by a farming family. There was a room in the house open to the garden where Delft tile pictures of cows and sheep hung. An old wooden cradle full of logs stood in a corner and in the centre was a mahogany table – a summer room, a room where we played, and the Crown Imperial lily with its foxy scent grew outside. The manor-house was old and worn and smelled of damp and skimmed milk. In a pale yellow room in the house where the floor boards creaked Margaret and I practised on an old and out-of-tune piano. It was cool and dark in that room and we haltingly played scales on the stained ivory keys. Not one ray of sunlight penetrated the room. It was a place of concentration and quiet and we enjoyed our times there, knowing the farmer's wife was at hand to encourage us as she scrubbed out her milk pails. At the back of the house was a large expanse of damp ground where willows and the flowers of cuckoo-pint grew. I found a wild duckling in the grass under the willows, in the swampy ground surrounded by the flowers which grew there. Its small body was like a yellow powder-puff and its wings were folded close to its body. Its half-shut eyes looked as though they were about to wake from sleep but its webbed feet were curled under, not stiff but as though it would not continue to learn to swim. Its beak was held tightly together, no longer wishing to search for weeds and small insects in the water where its mother would have led it. It was warm but I knew that it was dead. Its mother had left it. I carried it home with me to Maybrook and laid it in a box and put it on the nursery window-sill, leaving the lead-latticed window open, hoping that it might once more breathe. I forced warm milk down its beak and watched over it day after day. But it was stiff and its black eyes were glazed with grey. Then the flies came and the duckling began to smell. I would not part with it but my grandmother insisted that it be buried in the garden. I loved my duckling almost more than anything alive. But I was forced to cover it with earth in its box near to where I had found it. I did so with much crying and wailing. I had lost my duckling. I told myself that it corresponded to another duckling somewhere in the heavens – I knew. That day I no longer played 'The Jolly Miller' on the piano. I sat in the summer-room in a little rocking-chair, staring out at the pergola and the trees which were just coming to life.

*   *   *

The spring at Maybrook was unbelievably beautiful. Not even the war could spoil it. The garden smell, the joyful smell which seemed to hold promise for all our lives; the war could not kill this. The round-headed Portugal laurels were carpeted beneath with scillas and grape hyacinths; the unfurling sticky buds of the chestnut trees, the magnolia at the back of the house, and soon the pale yellow buds of the Mermaid rose would be opening on the grey stone wall facing the broad walk. In the wild garden where the stream ran, primulas were massed. The little Gothic building there, which looked like a church, had a wren's nest built inside. On the ponds ducks and moorhens nested beneath the branches of the weeping willows. We found hundreds of nests in the garden amongst the clipped yews. Thrushes, blackbirds and even 'the plain eggs of the nightingale' were there. We searched for the nests in the garden which was so large it seemed like the whole world to us. The sun shone on the lead figures called Beattie and Babs and coloured the grey lichen on the stone seats and the statue of Bacchus where the black fan-tailed pigeons cooed. In the fields of Dawthorne and Naboth the hawthorn trees would be in flower and the cowslips too. Violets grew in the hedgerows in the lanes.

There was a yearly expedition to gather kingcups or

marsh marigolds with Nan and Nan Offler and Margaret. It was a two-mile walk to the grey stone mill where the stream of clear water ran, where water-cress grew and swamp ground surrounded the River Nene. It was there we took our picnic to find the kingcups: the dazzling marsh marigolds with their hollow, succulent stems. They seemed to spread each year like a field of a cloth of gold. We went splashing in the water, picking as many as we could carry. They would brighten the nursery table for days after. Nan and Nan Offler and Margaret and I set out. Nan and Nan Offler dressed in their dark suits and hats; Nan in her white blouse and Nan Offler with her amethyst brooch pinned on her scarf at her neck. For the first time we would be allowed to wear cotton frocks made exactly the same, but mine had a yoke whereas Margaret's had a plain bodice. That did not please me. We also wore white socks and shoes which were soon blackened with mud. 'Ne'er cast a clout till May is out,' Nan Offler used to say. But Nan always had her way.

It was April 1942 when we set out towards the mill by Ashton Wold. Before we reached the War Memorial for the First World War, Nan and Nan Offler stopped and began to whisper to one another. Something had happened. I turned cold under the warm spring sun. I asked why we were waiting instead of going on to the kingcup field. It might get too late. Nan began to tell us a story of her childhood which was called 'The Pink Ticket' and one we loved to hear over and over again. But how could we listen at that moment. Soon it would be too late for the kingcups. At last we walked on but suddenly something snapped inside me. The sun went out and all the birds seemed to stop singing. From the church gate came several men carrying a coffin. The men and the coffin looked dark. The people who followed were dressed in black clothes. They all walked slowly in front of us, the men bending under the heaviness of the coffin. Their steps sounded in unison as they tramped on the gravel. They passed through the churchyard gate. Who was in the coffin and where exactly were they going to bury it? Oh, the sun went out and I wrapped my arms tightly around me. We had to wait until the cortège had passed and then we went on along the road where the almond trees were in flower, strewing the verges of winter grass with their pink petals as though some occasion had taken place. Nan talked all the time of the kingcup field but I picked none that day.

At night, lying in the dark oak bed in the night nursery, I woke up and screamed. I was petrified of what I had seen. A coffin, a long-shaped box with someone lying inside, to be buried under the ground. No one knew why I screamed night after night.

*   *   *

On a summer evening I was sitting with my grandmother on one of the garden seats which faced what they said had once been tennis-courts. That was before the war came. There were fourteen gardeners then but now there was only Mr. Loyd the head gardener and Alfred Titman the old man to help him. So the smooth green tennis-courts had become rough grass. Much prettier I thought than all those white lines and nets and people running about. Juno, the lurcher dog, lay beside us. She was a mad dog, frequently taking off and galloping in huge circles trying to catch her shadow or some imaginary hare. It was a Sunday evening; the sun was still quite high; Margaret and I had been to evensong in the church with our grandparents. The only sound was an occasional bee humming amongst the flowers. I thought of the hymns that evening: 'As pants the hart for cooling streams.' 'As pants the heart for chocolate creams,' we had sung loudly. Our grandmother never minded. We had sat on either side of her in the old pews, holding her hands to warm them during Mr. Clarke's long sermon. It was always cold in the church even in the summer. I sat next to the wall where there was a crack which looked like a spider. Opposite there was a brass plate set into the wall for our mother and there was a stained-glass window for our Uncle George who had died when he was six and a stained-glass window for our Uncle Victor John who had been killed in France at the age of eighteen at the end of the last war. Margaret could read what they said and I pretended that I could.

I leaned my head against my grandmother's shoulder. She smelled of a kind of lavender but she was not that sort of person. She was sporting and tough, enduring all weathers. These days she knitted for the Red Cross for the soldiers abroad. The hall with the minstrels' gallery was filled with scarves and socks and mittens. They were piled high on the refectory table. The portraits of our ancestors looked down on them. The bundles of grey wool garments contrasted oddly with the pearls in the frames of the miniatures in their glass cases, the Fabergé boxes and the rows of chiming watches. Margaret and I knitted too. We knitted garters. Five plain stitches of grey wool on the needles and then backwards and forwards again. It was not very interesting and mine did not look like garters although Margaret's did. Our grandmother knitted quickly without looking. We loved our grandmother.

I was thinking how much I loved her as I listened to the bees humming in the flower border on that summer Sunday evening. Suddenly she said: 'Oh, how forgetful of me. I have left my handbag in church on the pew. Do you think you could find your way there and fetch it for me?'

A shivering went through me at her words. Just suppose there was a coffin in the church? The church would be darkening now. The coffin would be placed by the altar and I would be alone with it. Shut in the church. I feared so desperately. But I had been trained to obey and not to show fear. I must not speak of fear. 'Yes, Granny.' That was what I had to say. I told myself that there would be no coffin but I was still afraid. I set off over the bank and walked down the broad walk threading my way slowly in and out between the conical-shaped yews. If I went through the bluey-green garden gate where the statue of Bacchus stood I might meet someone on the road who would come with me. But there was no one on the road on a Sunday evening in the village and if there was, our grandmother would know and she would think me a coward. 'Oh please God,' I said, 'make me not a coward.'

I ran as fast as I could, clenching my fists until I reached the church porch. I gripped the grey crumbling stone and traced the dog's-tooth pattern with my fingers. I grasped the latch of the door tightly between my finger and thumb. I pressed it down tentatively. The door creaked. There was no longer sun in the church. I did not look at the altar. I could hear my heart beating louder than the ticking of the church clock. I looked at the left of the nave where the tattered and threadbare regimental standards of the Life Guards jutted out in lines along the wall. They were from past wars and symbolized victories and defeats. I knew that my great-grandfather, grandfather, father and uncle had all commanded the Life Guards. I was proud of them but how could I live up to them? Underneath the standards lay a book with the names and photographs of all those in the village who had been killed in the First War. I loved the photograph of our Uncle Victor John. He was so handsome in his uniform as a young lieutenant. I now looked quickly at the banners which hung in dusty shreds and made my way to the opposite side of the church where we always sat. My grandmother's handbag lay against the crack in the wall which looked like a spider. I snatched at the heavy bag. I felt tears running down my face. Tears of fear and panic. I walked on tiptoe back to the church door. I did not mean to but I looked behind me towards the altar. I burst into sobs. I thought I saw a coffin lying there which was perhaps where our mother lay. I also told myself that there was no coffin, only the shining altar where it might be one day my place and my privilege to rest.

*   *   *

To some people the smell of freesias are intoxicating. For Margaret and me they were the start of a long and secret period of unhappiness. We were moved from May-brook. It was thought by our father and aunt that our grandmother and Nan and Nan Offler were spoiling us too much. They thought that we should live with other children. But we had no need of other children. We had need of Maybrook.

Our aunt's house was a long way away from Maybrook. The hall was filled with the smell of freesias. On our arrival I stood on one leg dressed in my tweed coat, smelling the scent which seemed to pervade everything. The light and sunshine and the smell of flowers in that house would have delighted most. But my heart broke. My spirits crumbled into a trembling nothingness amongst the light and the laughter and the flowers and the airiness. We had been taken away from our home which was full of the mystery of all things, even down to the tiny dark mark of my excrement which I had placed on the flower-patterned night nursery wall. Here there were sounds of other

21

children and unfamiliar noises. I stood for a long time in the hall with its black and white stone floor which was supposed to have come from Gloucester Cathedral. For this was an old house too, not Jacobean or Elizabethan but Georgian.

Our aunt was supporting many. Her own son and her sister Katherine with her children: Alastair and Daphne and Jane and Elizabeth. Katherine's husband had been killed early in the war. She had since married Alastair Murdoch who was away fighting in Italy. All we children shared a nursery with Nan and their Nanny who was called Nanny Mutt. Daphne was unhappy too, but we never spoke of it. Every one of us was shut and closed inside ourselves. Except to be naughty. I was the naughtiest of all. One Sunday I took Nan's scissors and with the help of Daphne cut into shreds everything I could see. The curtains, the rugs on the floor, our clothes and Jane and Elizabeth's baby dresses which were made of embroidered lawn. Before it was noticed we were taken to church and Daphne's conscience troubled her so that she burst into tears. I kept silent but afterwards I admitted that I had done it.

Once Alastair Murdoch came home on leave. He was extremely handsome. I stood at the top of the stairs to listen to him practising Scottish reels on the piano. Every evening he would play with his children and little Alastair and Daphne his step-children. He treated them equally. He danced Jane and Elizabeth on his knee and held them high in the air. Daphne sat on his lap and he read little Alastair and her a story. He did not want Margaret or me to sit on his knee or to hold us near him. I understood why he did not want us. His time was short, he might never see his children again so how could he have been expected to bother much with us? In that light gay house, what pain, jealousy and bitterness dwelt. I felt the continual anxiety

of the grown-up world. They had much to bear. I grasped
the glass lamp which had small raised spots all over it that
stood on a table in the drawing-room. The cool feeling of
the small raised spots gave a pleasant sensation in the
palms of my hands. It did something to soothe the pain
after big Alastair, as we called him, gently pushed me
aside.

Why was it that our own father who was also away at
the war, did not on his rare visits draw Margaret and
myself towards him?

Why did they not leave us at Maybrook, in the garden
there, near to our mother's grave?

Only a few weeks after big Alastair's visit we felt there
to be great trouble in the house. We were kept in the
nursery. The grown-ups had turned away in their grief.
Big Alastair had been killed fighting in Italy. Terror
struck me. I went to our bedroom, along the light sunny
passage. I stepped quietly on my toes so as not to disturb
anyone. The door of Katherine's bedroom faced me at the
end of the passage. It was open. I saw the reproductions of
Corot's paintings on the walls of her room. Their grey-
green trees seemed to move slightly as did the distant
poplars through the window. Katherine was kneeling by
her bed, weeping and praying silently for big Alastair.
He was the second husband she had lost in one war. I
stood, unable to believe what I saw. I stood there for a
long time. She did not know I was there. How could she
and the others bear it? I wished to run to Nan's arms and
to weep for Katherine. But I made myself go to my bed
and turn my prying eyes away from her grief and the
sorrow which pervaded that house of light and sweet-
scented pain.

*   *   *

One summer afternoon when the grown-ups were resting from their war work, Katherine and some of my cousins were playing croquet on the lawn. On the smooth lawn in the sun where the only shade to be found was under the cedar tree. I sat on the grass watching them. I did not wish to spoil their game so I waited for another round or for someone to grow tired and fall out so that I could take their place. I watched Katherine and thought how beautiful she was. At last the game came to an end. 'Can I play now, please?' I asked, thinking they would continue. Katherine threw down her mallet and my cousins did the same. 'It's all yours. You can have the lot now,' she said and walked away. How infinitesimal the situation was, but her words stung as nothing had before. I crept into the long grass, breaking through the thick stalks with the spittle of insects brushing my bare legs. I climbed into the hammock which was strung between two trees, hiding myself, terrified of pity for my weeping, and everything became dark in my convulsions of grief and yearning for my mother.

*   *   *

It was towards the end of the war when Margaret and I were taken with our cousins to London for the wedding of Katherine to her third husband. Everyone was glad for her and her children that they should once again find happiness.

We entered the church. The smell of incense was heavy in the air. We were all dressed in our best clothes. Jane in her pale yellow coat and bonnet. Daphne, little Alastair and Elizabeth. A great fuss was made of and adoration poured out to our cousins by all their delighted relatives. I was glad for them too and grateful to be included, but what bitter jealousy and envy boiled in me as Margaret and I stood there.

When the wedding ceremony was over we were taken back to the country in a large black car driven by a chauffeur in uniform. The car had a glass partition between us and the chauffeur. I sat on the thick padded seat full of anger and fear and resentment. Suddenly it became too much. Something snapped inside me and I fell on the floor of the car. With great will-power I could have stopped myself but instead I sank into a faint, almost a coma. I could still hear people's voices although I could no longer see. Everything was black, black, black. I thought that that was what hell must be like. On reaching my aunt's house I was carried up the stairs by the chauffeur. When I became fully conscious I was ashamed for spoiling a day of gladness when all those round me and the whole world had suffered so much. But I could not bear the apparent lack of attention and love from which I felt myself to be slowly dying.

After that it was early to bed with pills, when in summer the other children would still be playing out of doors, and I was excluded from any exciting events such as panto-mimes or the circus and the Victory Parade when the war was over. I knew I could not force love to come, but to faint brought me what I craved. Nan or my aunt would smooth my face and body. The caressing touch of skin on skin.

*　　*　　*

During the holidays the house was so full that Nan and I were moved to sleep in the high attics of the house. I had a little bedroom with a crescent-shaped window where I lay in fear, waiting to hear the ghost who was supposed to walk up and down the long passage. Nan and Nanny Mutt and Olive the nursery maid and Cuddy the house-keeper all declared that they constantly heard foot-steps above. The passage was so light but it was not happy.

It was in that little room that I developed measles and whooping-cough. I lay ill for days with a high fever, believing that I was back in the night nursery at May-brook, watching my Nan undress by the light of a night-light and letting down her thick black hair and brushing it all the way down her back. I thought I was at home again.

And then my illness changed into encephalitis and I do not remember any more. I was moved to a nursing-home where they thought that I would die. I was told that my aunt and Nan took it in turns to sit by my side, repeat-ing my name over and over again, trying to bring me back to life. When they thought that I might die my father was sent for and he was granted special leave from the Far East, where he was posted. During his stay I regained consciousness and I saw a man with a beautiful face stand-ing at the foot of my bed, who they told me was my father. I just remembered him as the man who had brought us a case of oranges, which we had never seen before, while we were at Maybrook. Margaret and I had sat far away from him, red in the face, so shy we were. He had also given us some special pocket-money for each of us to make our own garden. Margaret had planted seeds and watched for them to grow, but I had bought a beautiful rose bush which bore white flowers. I loved my rose bush but my father had written to say that I was lazy not to plant seeds like Margaret.

And here he was, my father, who had come across the world to see me. I was so proud and grateful that he should care enough. We did not touch each other but I loved him and each day he came to visit me I grew better. When at last he had to go, I was well.

*   *   *

Because of my delicate health I was sent to Maybrook for quiet holidays with Nan instead of going to what were considered to be more exciting places. How much I looked forward to those visits; to return to what I knew to be my home; the smell, the touch, the essence of everything I loved. I belonged there, and I was close to my mother who had loved it as much as I. Our grandfather had died in the middle of the war and now our great-uncle Bertie lived there with our grandmother. He was a small man, a retired admiral, who was fond of jokes which delighted me. So now I had him and my grandmother, Nan and Nan Offler all to myself. They were the happiest days of my life. Those days of freedom in the garden which was my paradise. It was my rightful place and I was alive as nowhere else. All unhappiness was shed as I searched in the garden for the nests of the birds of Northamptonshire, and made ballrooms in the boles of trees, patting wet moss on the ground and hanging daisy and buttercup chains above. I played cricket in the field known as Clarkes Close with the gardener's son. I fed Absolom, the white cocka-too, with sugar as he swung himself round on his perch. I stood in the passage with the high glass roof watching ing the great wheel turn and pump to make electricity. Backwards and forwards, to and fro, never stopping, chug clank, chug clank. I fingered the red velvet curtains in my grandmother's oak-panelled bedroom and tried on her jewellery. I ran in the dark house. I danced in the garden. I lived at Maybrook. It was everlastingness.

*   *   *

After the war Margaret and I went to live in Scotland with our father who had married again. Our father was almost a stranger to us and I worshipped him as a hero from afar. He owned four farms in Scotland and a large acreage of hill land.

One September afternoon, the same year as we had moved, I was working with him at the harvest at the farm called Camus. It was a sharp clear day and the sea loch stretched behind us at its deepest blue. The sheaves of oats lay on the stubble waiting to be stooked. My father and I lifted the heavy sheaves, one under each arm and stood them in fours together. The grains of oats rustled and the straw scratched our bare arms. At the farm house Mrs. Baptie, the factor's wife, was making tea for the workers: hot sweet tea to drink as we wiped the sweat from our brows. I was twelve years old then and proud to be working with my father. Suddenly a man, a stranger to me, came up the rough farm track towards my father. He handed him an envelope and stood waiting for a reply. My father opened the envelope and read what was inside. He then dismissed the man. The note was to say that my grandmother had died at Maybrook. My father left the field immediately to prepare himself for the long journey south to attend the funeral.

He left me amongst the stooks of corn. I stood stunned and silent. I knew then that Maybrook and my mother had gone for me. I was now to lead my father's life and that the mystery of that most precious life at Maybrook must be stored in my memory as the corn around me in the granary.

PART 2

... the marble eyelids are not wet
If it could weep, it could arise and go.
Elizabeth Barrett Browning

At the foot of a hill, below the drop of a high precipice, there stands a cross. A cross carved out of pink sandstone. The cross is in the heather and it is where my father's mother and father are buried. Their names are inscribed on the cross and on the back my father's name too, although he does not lie there. The date of his birth and death and the name of his regiment are written. The grave stands in a place where ravens circle; beside a steep stony track. Sometimes the land is covered in mist and at other times when the sky is blue, the cross looks over Loch Fleit, the sea, the hills and the arable land and the ruins of Skelbo Castle. In the spring when the violet butterwort grows beside the track and pools of dark water lie in the reeds, the ravens vanish and larks sing high in the sky. I have thrown my flowers on my father's memorial stone. Shall I ever stop throwing them?

*　　　*　　　*

Our father's new wife was called Anthea. Margaret and I had a step-mother. We liked her. She was quite young and tall and dark with a white skin and a face which had classical features. Her hazel-coloured eyes wrinkled at the corners when she laughed; and she laughed a lot in a pleasing way. She was still beautiful. She was what I had always wished for whenever I had been given a wish. Anthea had two sons. They were the same age as Margaret and myself. Their names were Esmond and William.

Esmond was a tall thin boy with a pale face and wavy hair like a young Chopin. William was beautiful. We were all to live together in my father's house in Scotland which was called Innisaonar. We were to be joined together in happiness with the war behind us and to forget the darkness of the past. My father was happy with Anthea. They spent most of the time together. Margaret and I and Esmond and William had been given separate sitting-rooms. Margaret and I made books of pressed wild flowers we had collected and Esmond and William smoked in secrecy making their wicker chairs creak as they laughed over their favourite books.

Together we were wary. What was expected of us? We wanted to but why should we deny and forget the mysteries of our births? We did not know our father. They scarcely knew their mother. They had spent the war in America. That Christmas we all tried to be happy. We knew that we must be happier than we had ever been. We were a new family but what was lacking in the strange four faces that looked upon one another? For a time we closed our eyes and forgot.

Snow and ice were everywhere. The sun shone in the afternoon during the short winter days. The sun shone brilliantly over the snow-covered hills. The beach was frozen to slide on. The waves of the sea made a line of frost. The carpenter made us sleighs and we tobogganed down the hills behind the farm which is called Thorbol. Anthea joined in our games, bringing us together. William and I became playmates, daring each other to an excess of naughtiness; William with his dark lithe beauty and his keen intelligence. We connived together. Esmond and Margaret kept apart. My father taught Esmond and William to shoot rabbits. He taught us how to handle a gun and then a rifle. I felt the smoothness of the barrels. I felt the kick of the rifle on my shoulder after I pressed the

32

trigger. My father was strict about fire-arms. Over and over he repeated the rules.

I made friends with the gamekeeper's daughters. Their names were Christine and Jean. Together we climbed a tall fir tree near to the gamekeeper's cottage. Over a hundred feet high. *Pinus Atlanticus glaucus*. Its bluish branches acted as a step-ladder to climb. Up and up we went to the very top where pigeons roosted. Barefoot on the snow-laden branches. Quick and laughing to the very top. It was a daring and fearless race. My father walked one day beneath the tree to which I clung, a hundred feet above him. I saw his finely-boned face tense. I saw my father, young and beautiful with his fair hair brushed back so perfectly cut, his clothes so immaculately made. I saw my father nervous and taut as he looked at me in my tattered tweed kilt standing barefoot in the snow. The next day the lower branches of the tree had been cut so that it could no longer be climbed.

Gently my father ordered us into our roles. We obeyed him as though under a spell.

*   *   *

During the holidays when we were all together we were taught how to develop our roles. Esmond became a keen fisher. He spent hours in his room bent over boxes of hooks and brightly coloured feathers, making his own flies to fish on the small River Carneigh or the sluggish River Fleit. William became a good shot and my father took him out shooting whenever he could. Margaret read her history books. My father taught me to cast a line on the circle of lawn outside the house and then presented me with a small trout rod. First trying with a piece of string, my father showed me how to tie a fly on a line. I practised it until I became expert. Margaret could never manage it. I bicycled to the same spot over and over again. To a small pool in the River Carneigh below Thorbol Farm. There I caught a brown trout and to my delight my father named the place 'Sarah's Pool'. One day I fell over a stone on the river bank and broke the top of my rod. I held the two pieces in my hands and burst into tears. What would my father say? I did not dare return home. As I bicycled along the straight, narrow road beside the alder wood I met Wallace MacLeod the postman, my friend and teacher in Gaelic. Seeing my red eyes and the broken rod he tried to comfort me and gave me the courage to go on home and report the news to my father. I found him in the gunroom which was dark, with the walls lined with rods, gaffs, guns and rifles. I held the two pieces of delicate wood in my hands and stood before him. I dared not utter. To my amazement he took my face in his hands. I could feel the bones of my face against the bones of his hands as though there were no flesh between us. He looked straight into my eyes. His eyes were a bright clear blue, not like mine. Mine were my mother's eyes: the colour of blue-black ink. He held my face firmly in his hands. I did not remember feeling his touch before. I feared it but at the same time it calmed me. He told me the story of how he, as a little boy, had been given a trout rod for his birthday by his parents. That day they went fishing on Loch Ness. They climbed into the boat and the first thing he did was to sit down where he had laid the rod and it had snapped in two. My father understood. For a moment we were equals.

Behind the house there is a larch wood. The larches sighed in the wind. A path led up through the wood and on the opposite side of the larches there stood a crowd of stunted birch trees. Around three birches my older cousins had built a house. That was before the war. The foundations of twigs still remained. On these foundations Christine, Jean, William and I built another house. We wove sticks through the twisted branches and filled the cracks with heather which we tore from the bare hill with our hands. The house stood firm on its foundations. To complete the house we covered it in wet green moss so that no heather could be seen. A burn trickled in front of the house. It was choked with decaying wood. I cleared the burn until the water ran fast again. I turned to see my father watching me approvingly, his black labrador dog by his side. He too liked to work with water. I formed a secret club with Christine and Jean and William. We chose names for ourselves like 'Seal' and 'Rowan'. We set up a tripod in front of the house and lit fires. In a billy-can we made sweet tea and in a frying-pan we tossed pancakes. We melted down an old lead pipe and poured the boiling liquid into moulds made of wet sand. The moulds were in the shape of spearheads. When the lead hardened we bound the spearheads to staves and found ourselves fully and freely armed. I kept our activities in a log-book in strict chronological order. I made each one of us write an entry about their own experience. Neither Margaret nor Esmond took part. They were too old.

One day my father became a platypus. He actually decided to become one. He ordered a platypus hunt. With our lead-headed spears we hunted him. Over hills and through the swampy alder wood. Christine, Jean, William and I. We gave the platypus ten minutes' start and he led us for miles and miles. We followed each clue he left. Deftly twisting and turning and going straight on, the platypus fled. With fury in my heart I hunted my platypus. He dodged me between boulders and birches and places where wild cats lived. With my spear I hunted him until the end.

And at the end I found my father sitting quietly in the

smoking-room at his desk, giving no indication that he had once been a platypus.

During the term-time Esmond and William were away at school. Margaret, too, had been sent to a boarding-school in London. I was kept at Innisaonar. Every day an elderly lady came from Dornoch, the nearest town, to give me lessons. I learned from her willingly. We did no French or mathematics or history or geography or any of the un-interesting subjects I had been accustomed to. She taught me to play the recorder and told me stories of Greek mythology. I began to search for naiads in the burns and dryads amongst the birches. I enjoyed my solitude and ran barefoot with a little black kid I had been given which I fed from a bottle. She followed me wherever I went. Her neat hooves pattered behind me. She learned to stand on her hind legs and to jump on my back when I crouched down. She skipped on to rocks and boulders waiting for me to go on down the hill and then she would skid side-ways as fast as she could until she had caught up with me. My father would not allow her in the house so she was tethered on the rough grass bank where I could keep an eye on her. I swam in Loch Fleit at the place where the great sluice-gates are. I felt the salmon slither round my body in the water. They jumped all around me waiting for the rain to come so that they could go on up the rivers. It was warmer to swim in the rain. Then I would return to my Nan who spent her time these days knitting clothes for me in one of the dark back rooms which looked over the yard. She now had a scar on her forehead which was the result of a train crash and her arm had begun to hurt. No one knew that her grave illness had begun. One day a picture in her room fell from the wall. She was unduly upset and said it meant bad luck. We cried over the fallen picture as if we both knew that we would not be much longer together. I always loved to go back to her although she looked disapprovingly at my bare feet. She would have preferred me in white socks and shoes. She knew I was no longer the little girl she had brought up and sometimes I was cruel to her. 'I have finished with you, ducky,' she said. Then I clung to her and asked her for forgiveness. After a time she gave in, although she wished I did not run so wild.

Anthea was preoccupied. She was soon to have a child. We had all known for long about this child so it was no surprise. She wore smocks over her skirts and I watched her grow fuller and fuller. She arranged vases of flowers in the drawing-room and made plans for the alteration of the walled garden. Anthea hoped for a girl as she already had two boys. My father, who so longed for her every wish to be granted, wanted a girl for her. So the child was known as Louisa long before it was born. My father was preoccupied.

One October morning at seven o'clock my father came to Nan. 'No one is to go through the swing doors in the passage until I tell them,' he said. At eight o'clock Louisa had been born. My father sent for me. I saw Anthea lying in bed, propped up by many pillows. I saw the bright sunny room with a blue sky blazing outside. I saw the new-born baby lying in her cradle. She was fair and pink and perfect. I was intrigued. I looked at my father. I saw him relieved from anxiety and pleased with Louisa. I knew then that things were all right. I left the room knowing in the depths of me that I was still his only son.

Three days after Louisa's birth it was my thirteenth birthday. My father gave me a kite. It was no child's toy. It was a proper yellow box-kite. He and I went down to the sea-washed turf on the shore of Loch Fleit and flew it. A strong wind blew. It was the back of an autumn equinoctial gale. I had my father all to myself and we flew the kite high in the sky. The pull was so strong that we both held the slat of wood as we let the long, long string unwind. The kite became smaller and smaller so that we could no longer see its colour. A black speck in the sky. We ran along the turf following it, both of us full of joy. My father's black labrador seemed to find the situation unnatural. She barked. After the kite had exhausted us we drove to Little Ferry. We sat on the old wooden pier. The tide had turned and the water was rushing out of Loch Fleit into the sea. We sat silently on the pier gazing into the clear water below us. At the bottom of the deep green water lay stones smooth and shining. As we sat close, our tweed jackets brushed together rough and vibrant.

I watched Louisa's progress during her first few weeks with intense observation. I watched the monthly nurse perform her duties. I returned to my room and acted out exactly what had happened with my doll. It was a china baby doll. I bathed it and fed it and wrapped it in its cradle and pretended it was my child. I did it secretly. I should no longer play with dolls.

After a month, preparations began to move south for the winter. My father had bought a farm in Oxfordshire where we were all to live except for the summer holidays. I did not want to go to Oxfordshire. I wanted to stay at Innisaonar. My father had chosen Oxfordshire because it was where Anthea had lived and most of her friends were there. I stopped watching Louisa and the monthly nurse and returned to Loch Fleit to fly my kite. The sea-washed turf was sodden with salty water. My bare feet made squelching noises as I ran. I caught a cold and was put to bed. My cough grew worse and worse. At times I could hardly breathe. The doctor said that I had a patch on my lung and that I was not fit to travel. To my fury, to my hatred and to my sorrow, my father, Anthea, Louisa and the nurse left me behind. I was sent to the local hospital and the house was shut. Nan was put in the Sutherland Arms Hotel in the village of Golspie. My father had abandoned me in favour of Anthea and Louisa. I cried in the hospital. Nan came to see me every day with Buddy, my terrier dog. She arrived out of breath, her lovely old feet pointing at ten to two. She then went by bus to Innisaonar to feed Puss, my black cat. Puss would be waiting for her at the bottom of the drive and would leap through the bracken up to the house to get her food. I did jigsaw puzzles with Nan but I cried when she left. It was the same every day. I was afraid of being alone and angry with my father. When I was better Nan and I with Buddy, and Puss in a game hamper, all travelled south. Nan was to leave me when we got to Oxfordshire. I did not want her to go. I did not want her to leave me in this strange place, this Cotswold house called Fields. When we drew near I noticed that there were no hills as at Innisaonar and the fields were flat, lying ploughed under a leaden sky, not like the sweeping fields at Maybrook. Flat fields and a straight gravel drive leading to an ugly house. My Nan went on her way and I went in through the front door. I bent down and pulled up my long woollen socks. I straightened my tweed coat. I pursed my mouth and picked up Puss in her hamper. I walked up the stairs, up to the top, to the nursery floor. There I met a young woman who was attending to Louisa. She tried to greet me, in a foreign accent, and to take Puss from my arms. I would not let her touch me or Puss. I would not speak to her. It was Nan who should be taking care of Louisa. I went into a little room and saw a bed prepared. My father came to me. I looked at the floor. He told me that I must get into the bed although it was the middle of the day. I closed the door and did as I was told. Puss would not settle on the bed. She was in strange surroundings. Another house. How I hated it although it was to be my home. I closed my eyes and crinkled them very tightly and tried hard to think of nothing.

*   *   *

Once again we all had to become accustomed to a new life. During the holidays my father could not stand the noise we made. He liked to be alone with Anthea. The house was not big enough for Margaret and me, Esmond and William to have sitting-rooms. My father had two rooms built on for us to the existing house. One for Margaret and myself and one for William and Esmond. They were square concrete boxes like prisons. Margaret and I kept to our cell and Esmond and William to theirs. We were only allowed in the drawing-room at certain times. Margaret and I drew closer again. My absorbing involvement with William had been brief. We stayed now in two separate parties as if to establish our own back-grounds and identities. Our sitting-rooms were faced out-side with Cotswold stone and Anthea bought climbing shrubs to grow up the walls to make them less austere.

We were still probing the ground around us at Christmas-time that year. On Christmas Eve we all sat in the drawing-room and my father read aloud to us Charles Dickens's *Christmas Carol*. It was a custom he started which was to continue each year. It seemed as though he were settling in more and more to the security he needed so much. The security which would enable him to shut out his past unhappiness: the death of our mother and the miseries of the war; of the deep loneliness he showed when he spoke of Cairo and Berlin. As I sat watching him read aloud beside the fire, I felt his sensitivity towards all beauty. It came through as if he wanted to express it in some way. But when he finally closed the book, a masculinity and a regimental authority clamped down upon him like a suit of armour in which he had not been born. I knew that my role was to wear that suit of steel beside him and to love the things he loved. Margaret's role was to be domesticated and feminine.

Anthea leaned back on the sofa listening to the tale. For the first time in her life she, too, had found security. In my father. He was becoming her rock and her joy. William sat near Anthea demanding her silent attention, demanding affirmation that she was his protective mother.

We were excited about Christmas and the Christmas tree. In the morning my father came to my little room while he was shaving. He wore his silk dressing-gown. He woke me by dabbing my nose with shaving cream and he lifted me up in his arms. He held me close for a second and I felt his warm body pressed against mine and I smelled a sweetness coming from him in my half sleep. He then dropped me down on the bed. I laughed and began to open my Christmas stocking in front of him. We all went to church as a solid family as we did every Sunday. My father gave everyone beautiful and appropriate presents. Christmas lunch was full of jollity as we set the pudding on fire with burning brandy and we cracked nuts and ate crystallized fruits. In the afternoon we took Louisa for a walk. We went along the wet roads surrounded by the flat fields. My father pushed Louisa in her pram, admiring his fair baby with her rosy cheeks. I kept as close to him as possible. William kept close to Anthea, pretending he could not walk. 'Support me, Mother,' he said, leaning heavily on her. Then there was Christmas tea with crackers and paper hats. I grew more and more excited as my father joined in the game of reading the riddles which we found in the crackers. He had a way of laughing like a young boy. It seemed that Christmas was to go on and on. After tea my father and Anthea went to the drawing-room. We were sent to our rooms. I burst out crying. Why did my father shut himself up just when we were having such fun? Margaret tried to comfort me by suggesting that we play tiddly-winks. But it was of no use. The house had become silent and my father had turned away from me on Christmas Day before I went to bed.

*   *   *

My father had bought a Welsh pony from a farmer in Scotland and I had ridden her that summer wherever I could go. She was named Peggy and she was perfectly made for the hills and to canter on mossy stretches of ground through the birch trees. She was now brought down to Oxfordshire in a horse-box by train so that I could continue riding and also learn to hunt. She was put into a loose box in the stable yard and was fed on crushed oats by Owen Jones, my father's valet and handy man. Her bay coat was clipped and her tail brushed and trimmed so that she took on an appearance fit for the show ring. My father took me to London and ordered jodhpurs, a tweed jacket and a bowler hat from a tailor in Savile Row. I was to ride and hunt like my mother had done, with the same exceptional courage and grace. It filled me with pride that I was the one to be chosen to represent my mother in my father's eyes. My mother had ridden side-saddle in a long habit and a black top hat and veil. In his bedroom he had a photograph of her sitting so gracefully with her long straight back upon a beautiful hunter. She smiles gently. At the bottom of the photograph he now added a photograph of me in my hunting clothes astride the polished Peggy.

For the first few times he accompanied me out hunting

on an old cob named Charlie. We rode to the meets sometimes three times a week. Peggy became fresher and fresher. She was no longer the quiet hill pony I had known. She shied at traffic and when we reached the meets her nostrils quivered and she trembled with excitement. She pulled hard at the bit so I could no longer hold her and I lived in fear of disobeying the laws of the hunting field. I felt my face tingle and grow red in the sharp air as we galloped towards a ditch or a stone wall. Peggy refused to jump. She approached the obstacle in front of her and then abruptly stopped and I would have a fall. I always remounted and went on again as I had to do. But I lost confidence and felt ashamed of myself. It was not done to show fear. I was not only a boy, I was also my mother. Occasionally, while I waited beside my father at the edge of a wood for the hounds to find a fox, I experienced what I was supposed to feel. The horses steamed and jingled their bits, otherwise all was silent. Then suddenly there came the bay of a hound and then another and another until the whole pack had joined in and they streamed out of the wood to the sound of the hunting horn. I felt a shiver down my spine at that wild gladness and at that primitive beauty. One day we were in at the kill and I was blooded on my cheek by the Master who presented me with the brush. I looked at my father. I was proud and honoured. The brush was cured by a taxidermist and the top mounted in silver. The name of the place and the date were inscribed and also my initials. I wanted to do the right thing and I hung it in my bedroom.

After a time my father said that I had learned enough to go hunting alone and that I could travel to the far-away meets by horse-box, with Owen Jones driving. I did as I was told. I did not allow myself to recognize my fear although each hunting day to me was one of enormous strain. My mother had not been afraid. She went in front of all the men and achieved more than they could. I must do the same. But at the meets I looked enviously at the other children in their velvet hunting caps. I saw them mounted on their shaggy ponies which never refused to jump. These children were quietly in control and enjoying themselves.

On late afternoons as I returned from hunting, my father expected me to rub down Peggy and to clean the saddle and bridle before I did anything for myself. Once Peggy turned on me while I was feeding her. She bit a piece from my eyelid. I got out of the loose box and stood shaking with fear. I realized then how afraid I was of her. But I must not, I must not show it. I went back to the house to the warmth of the dining-room. My father asked me what had happened when he saw my bleeding eye. I pretended it was nothing. As usual I ate my boiled egg for tea, which was my reward and treat, in total silence.

It was on one of these dark afternoons that I took my terrier dog Buddy for a walk. He yapped and deliberately disobeyed me. I took his leash from my pocket and began to beat him. He cowered in the stable yard and shut his eyes tightly. His ears which usually pointed cockily, one up and one down, laid low on his head and his white shirt front pressed against the gravel. I thrashed him again and again, fury and brutality mounting inside me. He moaned in pain. My anger was so great that I forgot where or who I was until I suddenly saw the gardener a few yards away. He had been watching me. I stopped thrashing Buddy but he still lay on the ground with his eyes tightly closed. 'Poor little dog,' the gardener said, his voice full of compassion. I stared at him and turned away, sobs choking me inside. I had given more than a punishment. I knew that I had sinned against heaven.

My father now owned five farms and did not know much about farming. He decided that he must learn. Because of

my health I was not to be sent to school. Instead it was
arranged that I have lessons with two girls of my age who
shared a governess. Every morning my father and I set
out to our different studies. He drove me to an Elizabethan
manor-house in a neighbouring village where the lessons
took place. He then went to spend the day at an agricultural college. He collected me in the afternoon and as we
drove home we discussed our day. It amused us both that
he had to go back to school and that we were students
together. We had homework to do and my father would
shut himself up in his study to read his farming books. I
climbed up to the nursery to sit with Mounette, the
Frenchwoman who looked after Louisa. I had at last made
friends with her and as she was very lonely we kept each
other company. Puss, my black cat, now lived in the
nursery during the day and at night she slept on my bed.
My father pretended not to like Puss. In his opinion cats
should live outside in order to keep down mice, or were
only fit for women to keep. He made hissing noises whenever he saw her and he called her 'Sarah's other self'. But
I knew that she had a place of affection in his heart
because she was the object of my devotion. It was my
habit to feed her at night at eleven o'clock. It was long
after everyone had gone to bed. I crept down the stairs
avoiding the ones which creaked. I made my way to the
kitchen and took some cold meat or a leg of chicken from
the larder and cut it into small pieces. I then returned to
my bedroom. Once or twice my father heard me and he
came out of his room and stood in the passage wearing his
pyjamas. Through the darkness I saw his face white with
rage. I stood in my nightdress in front of him looking down
at the tin plate of meat. 'Have I not told you before to
feed your cat at six o'clock before you go to bed. What do
you think you are doing, child?' He spoke so quietly that
I would have hardly heard his words had I not known

what they were. His frail presence was full of power, demanding obedience. After his words, his silence filled me with terror. I bent low over the plate. Would my father beat me for my disobedience? It was the knowledge that he would not which made me so afraid. His perfect self-control was fearful. 'Get upstairs.' I turned and went to my room in disgrace. Would he ever forgive me? I truly did not know. But every night I dared. I dared to risk it again. There was something that drove me to it. It excited me and Puss seemed to like her food at eleven o'clock.

*   *   *

Margaret and I often used to be sent to stay with our aunt in the 'house of light', where we had spent the greater part of the war. Now our uncle, our mother's brother, having retired from his regiment through illness, lived there too. We loved him. But in spite of his gentle and humorous presence and his connection with our mother and May-brook there was an unhappiness about our visits. We were very fond of our aunt and grateful for what she had done for us but our loyalties were split. I feared that she would take us away from our father, but Margaret told me it could not be so. On our return our father asked us if we had had a good time. That was all he ever said. We felt guilt and only murmured that it had been nice.

Fields appeared more promising in the spring and early summer. Anthea was making a beautiful garden; she was a gifted gardener. Long grass and buttercups sprang up in the two flat fields in front of the house and a herd of Friesian cows grazed in them. I grew excited as preparations to leave for Innisaonar began. My father could not tolerate the journey with so many people. He made the arrangements and drove to Scotland with his labrador dog, leaving Anthea to cope with the move. Owen Jones and his wife went in another car. A bus was hired to take us from Fields to Euston to catch the overnight train. There was Mounette and Louisa, Esmond, William, Margaret and myself, and Jamesina and Rayne, the Scottish housemaids. Then there were the animals: Buddy my terrier, and Tracy, Esmond and William's snapping corgi; Puss in her hamper, my mice in a box and my goldfish in a can of water. Also my budgerigars, Henrietta and Hamish in their cage, which was covered with a cloth to keep them quiet. My black goat, who had by now grown long horns and a beard, travelled in a pig crate.

After the long drive to London people stared at us as we got out of the bus at Euston. Mounette yawned and complained of a headache and Anthea usually lost something. When we arrived at Inverness early the next morning we all had breakfast in the Station Hotel. Then there was the next train to catch, to take us up the east coast for two hours to Meall station. The smell of seaweed and the sound of gulls filled me with joy as I jumped on to the little platform. And there was my father and also Owen Jones to meet us. We were driven in different loads to Innisaonar. Last of all came my goat. She leapt out of her crate into the back of the van, bleating loudly. My father did not complain as she dropped peppercorns on to the seat. I kissed my father and dared to put my arms around his neck. The move was over and we were going home together.

That holiday we were all given certain privileges. Margaret and Esmond were allowed to drive the old grey van up the hill road to Loch Buidhe. William, who was becoming more and more attached to my father, continued to shoot with him. I was given my mother's salmon rod. I treated it as though it were made of glass. Esmond drove me up to the top of the River Carneigh and left me there while he fished the lower end. We spent all day on the river, carrying our sandwich lunch in metal boxes in our pockets. I cast my line and again cast, watching the brightly coloured fly swing round in the rushing brown water. At the end of one day I caught a salmon weighing ten pounds, which was large for the little River Carneigh. I walked back to the road and hid the fish in the ditch. What pleasure it would give me to show it to my father. I walked along the road waiting for Esmond to collect me. Eventually the grey van came round the corner. Esmond had caught nothing. I told him about my fish and asked him to drive to the place where I had laid it. He did not and would not believe me. It was not possible that I could do better than him. He reluctantly drove to where I asked and I produced the fish. Esmond was silent, he looked furious. On arriving home I rushed in to my father to gather praise. Esmond went to his room and closed the door. After that he fished alone with an extraordinary perseverance which my father encouraged and acclaimed. But Esmond became withdrawn towards my father, and Margaret and I tried to avoid his increasingly biting tongue.

The boys sat in their room inventing their private jokes, and Margaret and I sat in our room doing our photograph books and listening to a record of a Wagner overture on the H.M.V. gramophone. It was the first piece of orchestral music that I had ever heard and there arose in me a passion which I had not known before.

I went for long walks with my goat, climbing rocks and boulders and wading through bracken which reached up to my chin. In the side of a rock face I found my shrine. It was a miniature cave, one hand high and lined in wet moss. The entrance was hidden by ferns. Water ran down the rock face and my shrine was dark and green inside. It was a thing of miraculous beauty which no human had seen before. I parted the ferns with my hand and stared inside the shrine. I went there every day. It was more important to me than anything. I felt it to be the place where the Virgin Mary dwelt and I came to ask forgiveness for my sins. Then I went to a rowan tree which grew out sideways from the rock face. I sat astride of it and thought about many things.

Margaret and I rowed in the shallow Meall Pool in a small flat-bottomed boat. The River Fleit runs into the pool before it gushes through the sluice-gates into Loch Fleit and on into the sea. A grey horse usually stands at the edge of the Fairy Island. Cowbells tinkle in the distance. In the middle of the Fairy Island bottles of plum and dandelion wine are buried. They are the remains of the distillery which William and I had made the year before. Margaret and I rowed up the River Fleit, plucking at the wild mint which grows on the banks. A hind and her calf leapt from under a tree. The tide had gone out. Margaret and I had to drag the boat over the sandbanks until we could float it again. We climbed back on to the road and raced on our bicycles back to the house, pushing them up the long steep drive making lines in the well-raked gravel. We had to be back at a certain hour for me to go to bed and for Margaret to make the salad-dressing for dinner. They were our father's orders.

My father went to cattle and sheep sales with the factor. Each farm was kept in perfect condition with never a stone in a wall out of place. My father worked hard and each of his employees knew what was expected of them. They were seldom asked too much. Gunn, the gamekeeper, was one of my father's closest friends. He was the most handsome man I had ever seen. He had come to Innisaonar as a boy and knew the hill as no one else. On shooting picnics he sat with the dog-boy a hundred yards from where we sat. His speech was full of fire but he worked with my

father as though they had been brothers. Wallace Mac-
Leod, the postman, came every afternoon on his bicycle
to deliver the letters. Afterwards he went to the kitchen
window to have a cup of tea. He propped his bicycle
against the fuchsia hedge and crushed it. He realized this
annoyed my father but having known him as a boy he
took the liberty and did it deliberately. My father wisely
ignored it.

Anthea had made another beautiful garden. It was
opened every year in aid of a Scottish charity. We sat on
the terrace in front of the house, tying bunches of flowers
to be sold and making buttonholes of white heather. Piles
of sandwiches were cut and teas were served under the
glass roof wash of the garage.

Anthea treated us all fairly without any discrimination.
She read a great deal, and practised the piano with her
unusually long thin fingers. She played with Louisa and
went for walks with my father. She helped entertain his
friends who came to stay and organized shooting picnics
which were held either in the freshly cleaned steading at
Skelbo Farm or on the hill. There, blue skies swept over
us, midges bit and the heather made a soft bed. Anthea
visited the wives on the farms. She worked hard in every
way to keep things as my father wished. I was not jealous
of Anthea because I liked to have a step-mother and most
of all I knew she was in a foreign land whereas I had been
there as an infant. But now I was more secret in my ways,
and I ran with my mother's binoculars slung round my
shoulder. And I knew each day that I became more, in
the eyes of my father, both his son and my own mother.

I always left Innisaonar in tears. Another whole year
before I would see it again. My father and Anthea went
there on regular visits but I did not. I did not wish to
return to Fields and the restrictions of lessons. That year I
watched the Meall Pool and the Fairy Island slide away

from me as the train moved on. My menagerie was with me. Puss in her hamper was by my side and my budgerigars in their covered cage were by the window. Before we reached Inverness a thud came from the cage. I pulled up the black cloth to look inside and there was Hamish lying flat on his back with his little claws curled tightly to his breast. He was dead. It was a catastrophe. In the sleeper train there came another thud. And there lay Henrietta beside him. Dead. I cried until I joined my father who was returning to Innisaonar for a few days. We wrapped up the little birds and I drew a map showing exactly the tree in the birch wood under which he was to bury them. I felt better when their grave was planned. First my father took them to the vet for an autopsy. It seemed that they had had a change of seed which did not suit them. He then took them north for their burial.

* * *

And so time went by. Fields, Innisaonar, Fields. Term-time, when all the others were away at school, holidays, term-time. Anthea started writing novels. She shut herself up in a tiny room with a typewriter. Her first novel was published. My father was pleased for her but he did not like her attention to waver far from him. However, he accepted that side of her and some of her more unconventional friends. But Anthea was to be cherished and also protected against a dangerous world of people of which my father knew little and deeply suspected.

Every year on April 1st, the date of our mother's birth and death, Margaret and I were taken by our father to her grave at Maybrook. It was a special day. A celebration and an outing alone with him. A day on which neither

Anthea nor Louisa had a place. A day when Margaret and I were alone with our father and mother. Spring flowers were laid in the back of the car and we would drive off to Northamptonshire. The hedgerows in Northamptonshire were usually bursting with green. When we reached the small town of Oundle all the familiar things flooded back. The swampy meadows of the River Nene, the elms standing solitary in the middle of the fields, the gypsy lane and the grey church steeple and spire of Maybrook rising in the distance. What utter joy it gave me to be home again. It was a different happiness from arriving at Innisaonar. It was the joy of being. We drove to the graveyard gate. The birds at Maybrook sang louder than they did at Fields, but they seemed to stop as we walked up the path to the corner where the family graves lie. At the head of our mother's grave there is a cross carved out of pink sandstone. Pink sandstone which had been quarried near Innisaonar, like the cross which stands on the hill. My father and Margaret and I stood on the white winter grass. My father placed the flowers on the grave. They shone white and gold. They gave life to it. We stood silently. My father plucked the grass which grew at the bottom of the cross in order to uncover the words: 'At the going down of the sun and in the morning, we will remember her.' Tears started streaming down my face. I could not stop them. I tried to behave like a man should behave but sobs stifled and choked me. I broke into hysterical weeping. I put my hands out for my father. I longed for him to take me in his arms and hold me as he would have held my mother. But he turned the other way. He pretended not to notice. Oh, how I needed his caress but he refused it. He could have made things all right but he deserted me in my greatest hour of need. I stumbled after him and Margaret into the church. We went to the family pew and knelt to pray. I wept and could not read the brass plates on the walls. As we drove away from Maybrook my father said to us: 'If I should die I want you to promise that one or both of you will come always on this day to lay flowers on your mother's grave.'

I do not remember if Margaret replied but I promised. Our father took us out to lunch in Oundle. It was to be a treat. I went with Margaret to wash my face and bathe my eyes. My father's mood changed back to his everyday self as though some burden had been lifted off him. Mine did not. I could not eat. I wanted to return to Maybrook. I was my fair mother who was married to my father and I was dead.

*　　*　　*

My mother had loved watching birds during her visits to Innisaonar. All the different kinds of sea birds and duck, heron, curlew, hawks, golden eagle and the little rare bramblings who live in the alder wood. My father had given me her binoculars, hoping that I would follow her example. He cared for bird life too and often stopped to watch small waders on the sand banks of Loch Fleit.

On a shooting picnic we had stopped at Loch Laoigh, a far-away loch in the hills. A pair of great northern divers appeared. We watched them from the shore, swimming slowly round the island in the middle of the loch, searching for trout. I was excited at the sight of such rare birds and I wished to share the moment with my father. We must keep silent so as not to scare them away. Perhaps they would continue to inhabit the loch and nest on the island. They glided so gracefully on the dark water. My father admired their beauty and then suddenly gave an order for them to

be shot. They were taking trout from the loch. Gunn went
to find the oars of the green boat, in order to prepare for
the hunt. I stared at my father. I could not believe what
I had heard. Loch Laoigh was a place where we went
perhaps once a year, owing to the distance and the small
size of the few trout to be caught there. To have the
privilege of harbouring these protected birds was an
occasion. They had arrived there from some far-off place,
either to visit or to make their home. I watched Gunn
pushing the boat into the water. My father refilled his
cartridge bag and started towards the boat. I went and
stood in front of him. 'You are not going to shoot them,'
I said. My father tilted his head back proudly. His chin
was pointed and his hair shone fair under the sun. A faint
breeze blew a lock of hair over his high forehead and
rippled the water. At our feet a single harebell trembled.
'Of course,' he said, 'they will eat all the trout in the loch.'
'What does it matter?' I wanted to shout but my voice
came out in a whisper. I shook with rage and despair.
My father looked down at me. Love was in his eyes. I had
proved myself again to be my mother and also I had pro-
voked him. What had begun for him as a vaguely dis-
tasteful task had now become a determined hunt for these
rare birds. I still stood in front of my father, not allowing
him to move on. For once I dared to lose my temper. 'No.'
My voice still came out in a whisper but I stamped my
foot. My father walked round me, got into the boat with
Gunn and William and headed out into the loch towards
the great northern divers. I turned sharply away, leaving
Margaret and Esmond. I walked and walked in the
heather. I walked away from the scene, away from Loch
Laoigh and away from the direction of home. I would
have nothing to do with it. Miles of hill stretched before
me. Then in the distance I heard two shots. The great
northern divers were dead, their beauty bathed in blood.

I ploughed on over the hill not knowing where I was going and with tears running down my face. For the first time I hated my father for his love of me.

Those days we often walked fifteen miles a day, shooting grouse over dogs. My father and his guests, Margaret and I and William. Anthea stayed behind to entertain the wives and if we stopped for lunch at a place possible for a car to reach, she drove to join us with a picnic. Mounette came sometimes with Louisa. Mounette loved Innisaonar. The country reminded her of her native Brittany. Esmond did shoot but he preferred to go off alone to fish in some remote place with Tracy his dog. He loved Innisaonar too. He wrote an article describing a day's fishing he had had and it was published in a well-known magazine. My father praised and encouraged him but Esmond looked more and more bitter.

We walked and walked over the hill in line. My father and Gunn were in command. Gunn had control over the boy who held the setter dogs and he worked the setters with a mastery which amounted to an art. When a setter pointed he stroked its head gently and murmured words to it. Stealthily the dog crept towards the grouse and pointed stiffly. The line advanced, the grouse were flushed and shots rang out. Occasionally a setter pointed at a toad and Gunn would curse the dog in crushing language. Sometimes I started thinking of other things and dropped out of line. Gunn admonished me. One day I fell back behind a little hillock. As I reached the top of it, my father who was a few yards in front, turned round to shoot. Before he saw me he had pressed the trigger. Shots blasted an inch away from my head. It was like a sudden rushing wind and I was hardly aware of what had happened. I saw my father standing there. Then he sat down in the heather. He lit one of the few cigarettes he carried with him. Everyone in the line looked bewildered and even Gunn did not rebuke me. He turned away and let my father confront me. My father did not speak. At last I fully realized what had happened. I studied my father's strangely curved mouth, twisted with his shocked and tortured thought. 'And so you nearly took my life? I would not mind to be your sacrifice,' I said to myself. There was silence on the hill for the rest of the day.

My father often took me on business trips round the estate as though he were training me, but he never offered me any explanations. He considered me to be too young. We drove towards Loch Buidhe to visit the shepherd and his wife in their cottage which is called Brae. It is up the rough hill road, miles from any communication. The shepherd asked my father if he could possibly have a bathroom built on to his house. There was the perfect space for one on the roof. The winters were long and cold and they only had a sink. We stood outside on the short grass which was kept mown by sheep. Wind bent the reeds. My father looked up at the roof listening to the man's polite request. At the end, my father shook his head. 'No, I am sorry. It would prove too expensive. At least seventy pounds.' I saw the look of disappointment on the man's face. He would have to tell his wife. But to my amazement he accepted my father's refusal as though it were justified. The man liked and respected my father as my father liked and respected him. I wanted to cry aloud to the sky at the injustice. How many times had Mrs. Campbell turned out her living-room with its polished brass, for us to herd into it as a shelter on our picnics? We took it for granted that we should use her house for our enjoyment. But my father had denied her a bathroom. As we drove home I did not dare rebel against my father. His love was too precious to be risked. I was, after all, only his obedient son.

*   *   *

Margaret and Esmond left school. Esmond decided to study law in order to become a barrister. I began to be increasingly nervous of him. I was crushed by his sharp tongue. In spite of his difficult character, William had become devoted to my father and was pliable enough to be moulded by him. This was not so with Esmond. From the moment of his mother's remarriage he had been jealous of my father's attachment to his mother. His hostility towards my father grew and grew. He seemed jealous also of Margaret and myself, perhaps because Innisaonar was more our rightful home than his. His feelings began to show in his face. He still had private jokes with William and they drove off together, when at Fields, to the nearest golf-course or pub or cinema. But they were not brothers in the same way as Margaret and I were sisters. They had not the bond and unity that we had. Perhaps Esmond was jealous of William too, for his beautiful looks which charmed everyone. It became so that everything Esmond touched at Innisaonar and Fields was contaminated by jealousy. His studies took him to London and he returned only for week-ends. I avoided him whenever I could.

One night I heard shouting coming from my father's study. Esmond was having a violent quarrel with my father. I ran to my room. I do not know what was said but Esmond never came home again. That night he left for good. He returned to his work in London and he joined a club where he made friends older than himself. There was in the air the feeling that on that night Esmond had committed a crime against my father. A crime of words and emotion which would never be forgiven. It was not spoken of. We seldom talked of him. Later we learned that he had become a devout Roman Catholic.

*　　*　　*

It was now considered that I was fit for school. At the
age of fifteen I had outgrown the seclusion of lessons in a
private house given by a governess with a Victorian way of
teaching, and also the childish games we played in the
hidden rose garden. There was a boarding-school for girls
in a large and ugly castle three miles away from Fields.
I was to be a weekly boarder. My father drove me there
to join the sixty other girls. I knew that I would see him
again the following week-end but when he left me it was
though he had abandoned me for ever. I was completely
unprepared for life at a boarding-school. Most of the girls
had been away from home since they were eleven or
twelve years old. They had their own friends and groups.
I could not speak to them. I could not make friends. I was
put into a bedroom with five others. One of them was a
powerful force in the school and she had a sarcastic and
cruel tongue. She made my life a misery. I was so homesick for my father. Having been taught by old-fashioned
governesses I was below standard, even for this un-
academic school. I entered a class with girls who were
slightly younger than myself. My only solace was work.
Work interested me. I listened to the lessons with great
attention. I learned everything that I could. Each week
I came out top of the class. My father praised me for my
reports and I could tell what pleasure it gave him. On
Sunday nights before my father took me back, I sat with
Margaret in our little sitting-room. I wept and wept. I
could not bear the shock and exposure of school life and
the dreadful homesickness. Margaret tried to comfort me.
She put her arms around me and I clung to her. But I
always had to return. One afternoon on a school walk, I
saw my father posting letters in the nearest village. I called
out to him but he did not hear or see me. Before I could
get to him he had driven away. The next day, without
anyone knowing I walked home to join my father. He

reluctantly drove me straight back again. I did not dare show to anyone, except Margaret, how unhappy I was. It was like the piercing of a sword inside me.

The death of Nan at her sister's home in the country was a loss from which I did not soon recover. Her death was not spoken about. I had no part in it. My father and Margaret went to her funeral. I was sent back to school. I remained speechless and rigid, mourning in secrecy for my Nan who I would never see again.

Every year the school gave a Nativity Play in the small village church. I was chosen to be one of two prophets. I had to stand on a hassock in front of the altar and speak the words from the Bible which concern the foretelling of the coming of Christ. I was told that the following year I was to take the part of the Virgin Mary, a role which was highly prized in the school and which would give me a certain status which I definitely lacked. I rehearsed my words as a prophet over and over again, so that I could not possibly forget them. I had failed to play the piano in the school concert because my hands would not stop shaking. For me, to do anything in public was a torture. The day of the play arrived. My father and Margaret were coming to hear me speak. I stood anxiously on my hassock. I looked along the rows of pews. I could see that they had not arrived. The time came. I spoke automatically without making a mistake. My father and Margaret crept into the church half-way through the play. My father had not heard me recite. He had not cared enough to arrive on time. He had not shared my achievement. Perhaps he did not love me any more. That night I went into a faint and then a coma. The authorities of the school were alarmed and I went home the next day. My father took me to a neurologist in London whom I had often seen before. It had been thought that I had grown out of my attacks. I did not tell the neurologist that my father had

59

failed to be with me on a very important occasion. I returned to the school with small white pills which my father gave to me every night when I was at home. He watched me until I had taken them. I was told that the following year I was not to act in the play. The excitement had proved too much.

I had now grown tall enough to ride a proper hunter. My pony was too small for me. My father bought me an awkward-looking horse which had belonged to a whipper-in. The horse's name was peculiar: Paintbrush. Somehow it suited the ungainly animal which I feared immediately. He had been ridden and hunted by a strong man and had been used to rough treatment and being near to hounds. I could not begin to hold him. He started to gallop and I could not stop. I was terrified. But I had to go on hunting. I had to live up to my mother for my father's sake. If I failed to do so he would love me only in an ordinary way, and that I could not risk. One day out hunting Paintbrush bolted. He galloped on and on. I saw a high fence of barbed wire ahead of us. Paintbrush jumped it and landed in the ditch on the other side with me underneath him. Somehow he did not crush me and we both came out unharmed with only the bridle broken. I rode home immediately and went to my room so that my father would not see me shaking. Later he was told by a neighbour what had happened. Before the next hunting day I longed for a hard frost so that the meet would be cancelled. The frost did not come. The ground remained soft and the weather mild. I got dressed for hunting. I walked down the stairs. I met my father in the hall. I was so afraid of what might happen that I could go no further. I clung to the banisters and wept. I wept in front of my father. The fear, the terrible fear of that horse and of the hunting field overcame me. My father understood. He forbade me to go hunting. I went with him to his study in shame. He told me that I had come to a cross-road. Either I give up hunting alto-gether or I must go to Ireland to a riding-school to be taught to ride properly. I then would be given the hunting clothes of a woman instead of those of a child. It was for me to decide in my own time what I was going to do. I stared at my father and asked his forgiveness for what I had done that day. He did not reply.

* * *

During the summer at Innisaonar, Margaret and I did not join the shooting parties as often as we had previously done. Instead we went for long walks together over the hill. We often stayed out all day. We walked far apart, a hundred yards or so, each of us deep in thought, making our separate ways over the heather and the patches of pink and green sphagnum moss. We went through the reeds and drifts of cotton-grass and over the swards of grass where the ruins of crofts and byres lay, left over from the Highland Clearances. We never disclosed our thoughts to each other. We had our different dreams and secret lives. Our lives were secluded, held fast by our father who protected us from the realities of the outside world. Mar-garet was shorter than me, and sturdily built like a small Shetland pony. I watched her striding over the moor, her thick hair bleached by the sun and her skin glowing with health. I watched her imperturbable step and envied her for her strength. She had the same coloured eyes as our mother but her face resembled more our father. It was said that we looked alike but my father insisted that there was no difference between me and my mother. I was tall and thin with a pale face and my tread over the hill was more intrepid. I was dependent on Margaret. She was the older and she had guided me since the death of our mother. We had clung together. We loved each other.

And then we would come together on the hill. We rested side by side. We lay half-naked deep in the heather. Our secret lusts knitted us closer than we had ever been. She was a young girl and I was a young boy and we sinned under the vastness of the sky. We did not speak and we had no confessor.

A stag came down from the hill one day and had been seen in the alder wood. My father took me with him to stalk the red deer. In a clearing, in an open ride, a few hundred yards from us, the stag appeared. It stood still with its great head held high trying to catch our scent in the air. But there was not a breath of wind in the wood and so it delayed its departure. I lay on the ground close to my father, our bodies pressed together. I trembled with a terrible excitement, feeling the warmth of his body as he looked through the sights of his rifle. The single shot cracked. The stag stiffened and fell. Again and again the noise of the bullet echoed through the alder wood over the stag's barely dead body and with its antlers dug into the ground. The stag lay under a Caledonian pine. My father and I stood up and together we approached it with a joyful sadness.

To please my father I still went fishing, but these days I took a book with me and hid it underneath my coat. One afternoon on the River Fleit, when the wind had dropped and the water was without a ripple, I lay on the river bank with my rod beside me and began to read. The air was hot and stifling. Spiders wove their webs in between the branches of the trees and flies buzzed round my head. I was alone with my book. I read on and on, forgetting where I was, when suddenly I heard a soft tread and I looked up to see my father standing above me. I had had no idea that he would appear. I pulled myself on to my knees. I felt my face go red and at last I looked up at him. 'That is not what you come to the river for,' he said quietly. In my shame I could say nothing. But I saw in his eyes a flicker of disappointment. How hard I tried to strive against that look. But the dam I had built in our river was slowly and gradually crumbling, and I could not stop it.

*   *   *

Anthea tried very hard to grant me things which my father considered unnecessary. We were all to go to a cousin's wedding in London. It was an occasion of great importance to us. I imagined myself in a new outfit of clothes, dressed as an elegant woman. My father said: 'Nonsense. The child can wear what she has got already.' That which I had already was an old blue coat of Margaret's which we called 'the policeman's coat'. I had brown lace-up shoes and a nasty little pink hat. I was not going to be outshone by Margaret. I insisted on high-heeled shoes and a large brimmed absinthe-coloured hat. The image of myself was clearly pictured in my mind. Against my father's orders, Anthea took me shopping. We searched every shop in the nearest large town for an absinthe-coloured hat but none could be found. There were green or yellow but the shop assistants shook their heads when I asked for absinthe. They did not seem to understand. Anthea looked exhausted after the day's shopping and we returned with only a pair of red shoes which bruised my feet and toes. That was one of many fights which Anthea fought for me against my father.

On a sunny day at Fields when William and I were on holiday and everyone else was out, we decided to have a tea-party on the lawn. We set up a table and chairs, and spread a fine white cloth over the table. We used the silver tea-pot and cut thin cucumber sandwiches made with brown bread. We had the setting for another grand occasion. We sat under the apple tree. William wore a collar and tie, and I my best dress. I did not feel very comfortable nor, I think, did William. We made formal conversation. After a while William said, speaking with difficulty: 'Will you marry me one day? Would you ever wait for me?' Whether he meant it or not, I was overcome that my long-known and beautiful William should ask to marry me, and after a pause I answered: 'Yes.' Then immediately I knew I had told him a lie. I could not possibly accept his proposal because if I did, what would I do with my father? He held priority over all else and he was my betrothed. The sun went behind a cloud as I shook my head and the sound of crunching gravel showed my father had returned. He had come to end our party.

After my sixteenth birthday I was taken away from the school near to Fields and was sent to an establishment in Oxford, run by a Swiss-German woman who was known by her pupils as Cuffy. She lived in a house in Merton Street where six or seven girls went to study French literature, history and art. Cuffy lived with a life-long companion who was also known by a nickname: Foxy. Foxy was an old man with thick white hair. He had great strength of physique and character, and tolerated the presence of the girls for Cuffy's sake but regarded them, save for exceptions, as a nuisance. He was an art collector and he owned a house in the High Street where he kept most of his treasures.

My father took me to Oxford for the first time. Louisa came with us. Cuffy, my father, Louisa and myself went into the front room studio which looked out on Merton Street. There was a large grand piano in the room, and an ancient gramophone with a horn. My father sat in his exquisitely made clothes in the room in Merton Street. Although he was not an academic man, he was never out of place and I sensed that Cuffy took to him. He was obviously the kind of Englishman and father that she liked. Cézanne water-colours hung on the walls which I noticed but my father did not. I felt strangely at home there although I stood in awe of Cuffy with her quick tongue and perceptive eyes. Her two poodles, whose names were Roistey and Grummy, lay in the studio. Cuffy made the little black Grummy play the piano for Louisa's amusement. He perched on the stool with his paws on the keys and performed his trick. Louisa laughed and Cuffy called her 'La petite'. When the time came for my father and Louisa to leave I wondered why I had not more of an urge to go home with them. I felt guilt towards my father that this place interested me and that I wanted to find out more about it. I looked once again at the Cézanne water-colours and they enraptured me. Cuffy took me upstairs to my room which I was to share with another girl. She left me for a moment, and I studied the pictures on these walls. They were oil paintings signed 'Frances Hodgkins'. Large blobs of paint stuck out from the canvases. I found them irresistible. Quickly, before Cuffy could return to the room, I picked off one of the blobs from a valuable painting. I was there to learn about art in all its forms and I was ignorantly entering a new sphere into which my father could not join me. My father had allowed me to take my first step on dangerous ground without knowing that he had done so.

The days with Cuffy were full. There were seven girls and myself. We were constantly working and occupied. Sixty French words had to be learned each day and written in an exercise-book. We sat round a table in a room which had a tapestry covering the wall. Roistey and Grummy lay under the table as we struggled through Racine and

Corneille. I was below standard, having come from a
school where the French mistress taught from books meant
for twelve-year-olds. I found everything extremely hard
but from the first day I sensed that Cuffy was a teacher
of genius. As she read she pronounced the words as though
on a stage and she acted out the sentences. '*Honneur,
gloire, devoir.*' I understood and was excited. Our essays
had to be written in French. I could not manage it. Cuffy
had to tell the other girls in private that I was not as
stupid as I seemed. We read *Madame Bovary* and were
helped into experiencing her emotions. I was swept away
by the romanticism of Chateaubriand, and for the first
time realized how small I was from the writings of Pascal.
Doors were opened every day into a new and beautiful
world. I entered each with full force and a determination
to understand. In the evening I was near to the shore of
drunkenness with what I had learned that day. Baudelaire,
Rimbaud and Verlaine. How could they all be possible?

Dinner was held at a long table in the dining-room with
Foxy sitting at the head. On rare occasions in the evening
he read poetry to us. He opened a copy of Ezra Pound's
Collected Poems and turned to 'La Fraisne'. Very slowly, in
his deep rolling voice, he began: 'For I was a gaunt grave
councillor, being in all things wise.' He held me under a
spell. But I was afraid of Foxy. When it came to be my
turn to take him his after-dinner coffee I did so with a
shaking hand. He had known Anna Pavlova and Nijinsky
and Diaghilev. How dare I speak to such a person?

We were not allowed to play the gramophone in the
studio without Cuffy's supervision, and radios and jazz or
popular music were forbidden. The gramophone with the
horn had a wooden needle which had to be sharpened
with a special instrument every time it was used. Cuffy
put on a record and through the horn with a wondrous
tone came the floating and dancing sound of a Schubert

Impromptu. What joy I was discovering. We went to lectures at the University amongst the undergraduates. Lord David Cecil spoke on Jane Austen in his high-pitched voice, bringing her and her characters alive as he twiddled his thumbs throughout the lecture. Julian Bream gave a guitar recital at Balliol and Bernard Shaw's *St. Joan* was played at night outside in a quad. I went for piano lessons with a very old lady who lived in Wellington Square. I was not worthy of her teaching; she had been a friend of Brahms and each hour was one of inspiration. We were let off homework which was known as our '*quotidien*', to go to Magdalen Chapel on Sunday evenings. In winter the chapel was lit by candles which made the red cushions glow and the choir boys sang anthems by Purcell and Byrd.

There was domestic work, too. After each meal we helped Ursula, the German cook, to do the washing up and every week we cleaned the silver. On Wednesday evenings we were allowed out with an undergraduate if invited, and the hour of our return was strictly noted. It was fashionable to be in love. Letters were dropped through the letter-box and our hearts beat fast as we ran to examine the envelope. Who was it for? Whose writing was it? And which college emblem was stamped on the back? I fell in love with an Irish Belgian scholar with a biting wit who played cat and mouse with me and complained that I did not speak. We were engrossed by undergraduate life and humiliated when we were reminded that we were only schoolgirls. I suffered at parties where I could not utter and stood and stared at Enid Starkie showing her red flannel petticoat. Occasionally Cuffy asked one or two young men to dinner but only, as she mockingly put it, if they were '*un jeune homme de qualité*'. We went for many walks and picnics. We punted up the river as far as 'Mesopotamia', and climbed Magdalen

67

tower at dawn on May Day to hear the choirboys sing. We went to the Bullingdon point-to-point and watched one of our friends from Christ Church lead the race. He was Joint Master of the Bullingdon Hunt and we thought that he would win. But at one fence he fell and his body lay on the ground, paralysed for life.

I took confirmation classes with the chaplain of Wadham College and was confirmed in a white dress and veil. My father came to watch me and he gave me a beautifully bound leather book of Holy Communion. The next day at eight o'clock in the morning I walked through newly fallen snow to Christ Church to take my First Communion. My father told me that Holy Communion had been of great importance to my mother.

Soon afterwards I fell ill at Cuffy's and was sent to bed with a high fever. As I tossed and turned with sweat pouring off me, it seemed that I was fighting a battle. I still had to make the choice whether or not to go to Ireland to the riding-school. I had not yet given my father my decision. During days and nights the riding-school stood before me, a horrific reality. I feared and detested the idea. It loomed up at me out of all proportion. I would have to go in order not to let my father down, but how could I do so? I had discovered a new world; the gate was open for me to follow a path which, before, I did not know existed. The inner life fought against the outer. I was torn in two. I could not talk about it to anyone and it tortured me. In my feverish mind I saw a picture of the riding-school with the instructor shouting at me, and then the cool abstract greenness of a particular Cézanne water-colour closed over me in sleep. When my fever had subsided I knew what I must do. The urge was too great. I must continue to follow the glimpse of that which Cuffy had shown me. My year with her was at an end and I wept at my departure. I knew that I had been one of the privileged, and I must now go on my own way. The door of Merton Street closed behind me.

At home I told my father that I would prefer to study music than to be sent to a riding-school. He accepted my choice with respect. He now knew what was to come. My physical appearance remained the same as my mother but he nurtured me as a changeling.

I was sent to Paris for three months in order to practise my French. I went to live in the flat of Mounette's mother near to the Parc Monçeau. Madame Bastet's dead husband had once known Proust and Richard Strauss. The flat was old-fashioned and the blinds only drawn back in the salon on Sundays when her relatives came. Her relatives sat in a row on small chairs, and they all wore tight-fitting leather gloves. Madame Bastet spoke no English and very little French. At dinner, which was served by Marie the maid, she would tell me how much she hated the Germans. She had lived through the occupation of France and it was her main topic of conversation. We had little or no communication except for the times when the blinds were drawn back in the salon and Madame Bastet and I played duets on the piano. But her fingers were old and stiff and my sight-reading bad, so we did not make much progress. We knew that we liked each other and apart from that she left me alone. I was in a foreign country for the first time but I was not lonely. I led a secret life. My father and Anthea came to visit me. My father looked so English in his bowler hat, carrying his rolled umbrella. I did not tell him what I did and I walked by his side with my eyes cast down, dependent and demure. He did not know that I roamed all day and most of the night alone in Paris, and that I rarely spoke to anyone. I attended some lectures at the Sorbonne and ate cherries for lunch in the Jardin du Luxembourg. I went to all parts of Paris and spent long hours in the cemetery of Père-Lachaise. I stayed too long searching for the grave of Alfred de Musset, laying a flower on Chopin's tomb and finding the place where Eugène de Rastignac in Balzac's *Le Père Goriot*, climbs up the steps to declare to the society of Paris below him: '*A nous deux maintenant!*' I spoke the sentence out loud in a rebellious voice. It was as though I were shouting it to my father. Late evening came and I got locked into the Père-Lachaise. My companions in Paris were the dead. I rapped at the door of the gate-keeper's lodge. The gate-keeper let me out and I walked back in the dark. I was without fear and I was free and independent. I spent all my pocket-money on seats for the Opéra to watch Serge Lifar dance in *Icarus*. I went over and over again. Late at night I lay on my bed imagining that I saw Nijinsky dancing in front of me in *Le Spectre de la Rose*. I wandered by day and night amongst the chestnut trees, living and bringing alive all that Cuffy had taught me. I went to Bourges by train and thought about *Le Grand Meaulnes*. I was on my way to visit a sister of Mounette's who lived in the forest of Tronçet. I took the wrong train from Bourges and found myself in Nevers. I returned by bus and was dazzled by the fields of mustard in that enchanted country. Monsieur Thibaud, my host and head forester of Tronçet, picked me a bouquet of carnations from his garden. I thanked him for his *oeillades*. He laughed, and realizing my mistake I blushed and could not look at him again.

It was not until I wrote to Margaret telling her about my life that my father grew to hear of it. He sent me the sternest letter I had ever received from him and also one to Madame Bastet. He threatened my immediate return. I was not allowed out any more alone. I had to be chaperoned by one of Madame Bastet's daughters. Paris lost its magic for me. I was no longer free and I looked forward to returning home.

TO THE PLACE OF SHELLS

Crossing the Channel on a rough sea, I realized just how homesick I had been, and I longed to bury my hands in the earth of England and to feel my father's arms around me once again.

*   *   *

It was not that we were forbidden to have our friends to stay. On one or two occasions we had tried it and both times it had been a failure involving such pain and embarrassment to Margaret and myself that we swore we would never ask anyone again. It was easier to invite girls. With them the strain was not so severe. But with men it was impossible. Our father did not allow them to sit in the drawing-room. We had to take them to our little sitting-room, and try to entertain them by ourselves. We felt awkward in doing so, ashamed at being treated like children and afraid the young men might feel trapped at the isolation. We wanted to be included in the family and to be treated as grown-ups, but our father did not allow it except at meals. Usually he did not like our young men and we were not encouraged to bring them home. We ceased to ask if we might. We did not want to go through the ordeal ever again.

It was on a pouring wet day at Innisaonar and I was looking out of the dining-room window while we were having lunch. Suddenly I saw a figure wearing a kilt walking up the drive. As he drew nearer I recognized him to be a friend of mine, a Russian undergraduate from Oxford. He was arriving unannounced, soaking wet and bedraggled. I dreaded telling my father. I had no time to do so. He made his way through the front door, his boots squelching and his hair all over his face. He had walked all the way from the west coast in the mist and drenching rain. He stood with his back to the fire in the drawing-room holding out his kilt for it to dry. It steamed from the warmth of the fire and his round face beamed at his accomplishment. He was very clever but his behaviour was always outrageous and he even annoyed his fellow undergraduates. I was pleased to see him but I had no idea what to do with him. My father looked at him with hostility and was icily polite. Anthea asked him questions as to where he had come from and whether he had had anything to eat. He was fed and shown to one of the little back bedrooms. His laugh could be heard all over the house. He said he was exhausted and he went to bed. Then he found his way to the nursery and persuaded Mounette to look after him and to take his temperature. He decided that he was very ill and returned to bed. Trays of food were carried up to his room. My father was furious. He went himself to take his temperature. The thermometer read normal. My father ordered him to get up at once. Very soon after he left, his laughter resounding behind him at the enormous joke. My father pushed the incident aside and closed it by saying: 'Just one of Sarah's foreign friends.'

Every year the meaning of Innisaonar changed for me. Margaret and I now went on separate walks. I often went up the steep track to the grave on the hill and sat there staring for many hours at the stretch of heather and marshland which lay between me and Loch Tarvie. I could not tell whether the distance was long or short. The stretch of land appeared to me as a mirage, a fairy place, where if I trod I would find no ground to hold me. It fascinated me. I dreamed all day and troubles mounted inside me.

We were now allowed to sit in the smoking-room after dinner. We played our father's old records on the radiogram. He enjoyed hearing them. Anthea sat doing her *gros point.* At her feet she had a footstool and my father would put a cushion behind her back. He treated her so delicately. That year my father looked through his old photograph books; and for some minutes Anthea was excluded from the scene. My father looked at photographs of my mother. I heard him sigh as he closed the book. I watched him with pleasure. My mother was still close to his heart but was it not dangerous to arouse the past in such a way? I looked at my father in his green velvet smoking-jacket which he wore for dinner. I looked at his porcelain-like hands as they closed the book which was full of pictures of my mother's gentle face. My father threw his head back. It was a gesture I knew so well. It seemed proud and also arrogant but it was not. In spite of my fear of him I guessed he was a nervous and an emotional man. I took advantage of his vulnerability. At that moment I knew that he was in love with me. A record played 'Dancing in the Dark', and I dreamed a dream.

A novelist lived on the other side of Little Ferry, not far from Innisaonar. He was more of a friend of Anthea's than of my father's. He rode everywhere on a motor bicycle. One day he came to tea. He wore a beautiful blue tattered kilt and a scarf was twined round his head. Margaret and I were slightly afraid of him and of his wit. He made us feel uncomfortable. But on that day to our delight he crashed into the rhododendrons on his motor bicycle. His scarf and kilt went askew and he made a large hole in the bushes trying to extricate himself and his machine. Margaret and I and William had to rush indoors so as not to show our laughter. We laughed and giggled and laughed and we could not stop. That night at dinner we sat round the table with some of my father's friends from his regiment, and their wives. Without knowing what I was doing I found myself speaking out very loud to the whole gathering. I told them about the motor bicycle incident which they had missed while they had been out shooting, and how funny it had been. Usually I did not say anything at the table but now I was laughing to my audience as I told them the story. When I had finished there was a hush. I looked anxiously round the table. Some of the faces were on the point of smiling when my father broke the silence in his quietest and coldest voice: 'I am not at all amused. How dare you laugh at his misfortune. Keep silent, child.' I went red in the face and stared at my plate. His words crushed all my life from me. I had thought that he would think it funny too. I had made a terrible mistake. A sobbing came from deep down in me but I fought it back. I sat through the dessert with sweat pouring from me and time seeming endless. At last I could leave the table. I went to my room and lay on my bed and the dam broke inside me. I cried with my whole body. All the defences I had tried to build for so long were swept away in the deluge of my tears. I saw for the first time the tragedies and sorrows of the world. The sadness of situations concerning people I loved, which I had not seen before. I wept for my mother and I wept for life. My father came to find me. He said that I could only cry if I had a reason. What was my reason? I could not tell him. I just wept and wept. He grew annoyed and went away. Anthea came to see me. She touched me with her hand and said: 'It is all right, you are nearly grown-up.' My father came again and demanded a reason. I became hysterical and everything went black. My father deserted me and I wept all night.

The next day was my eighteenth birthday. I looked at my face in the glass. I saw myself swollen and disfigured. But I had to try to appear normal. It was my birthday, a special day when my father and I were together. My father gave me a camera. I went with him and Margaret and

Louisa to the Shin Falls. We watched the salmon leap and listened to the roaring of the water. I limped through the day, hiding the wound inside me. The previous night was not mentioned. But as we drove by the side of Loch Buidhe, I said to my father: 'Please forgive me.' I watched his profile. It did not move.

The days which followed were like days spent recovering from a long illness.

*   *   *

Margaret and William and I were jealous of Louisa. She had grown into a pretty but spoiled little girl with fair curly hair and hazel-coloured eyes like those of Anthea. Mounette adored her and did everything that Louisa wanted. Louisa bullied Mounette and hit her with a stick. She now went to a little day-school in a village near to Fields and Owen Jones drove her there every day. Although he was so strict with us, my father gave Louisa all that she wished. He allowed her to sit in the front of the car while a grown-up sat in the back and he took her for walks alone on Sunday afternoons. He called her by a nick-name. Topsy. We were hot with jealousy at the privileges she was given.

Margaret had been allowed to go to London to work. My father disapproved but did not stop her. She did not eat enough in London and she fell ill under stress. She returned to live at home to help with domestic things and to enjoy a country life.

On leaving school, William was sent to do his military service in the Life Guards.

I went to London to meet people at parties as Margaret had also done. I detested the idea but because I loved to dance I did what my father expected. It lasted three long months. Three months of empty living, learning to be a lady, dressing to be pretty in new long ball-gowns, and drifting from dance to dance, and from one marquee to another. Dancing in great houses in the country where the staircases were strewn with rose petals and the gardens flood-lit. I drove back to London with young men through leafy lanes with the birds singing in the dawn. They took me safely to the house where I stayed which belonged to a gentle lady who saw that I returned each night. I danced and danced and danced but I made no friends, which was what I was supposed to do. At the dinner-parties I hoped to be seated next to the fathers of the girls. I found them more interesting than the young men. Once I danced with my father, just us two in the middle of the floor. We danced a waltz, forgetting the spectators, forgetting all as we danced round and round, my dress floating up, all the colours of the sea. It was a time for forgetting.

And I turned from the young men who wanted to kiss me. 'Why are you always so far away?' one of them asked. I had danced with him all night and he wanted to embrace me but I looked at him with cold and distant eyes which said: 'Now take me to my father.'

And so I returned to my father and I captured him by pretending that I was a beautiful woman with the walk of a queen.

*   *   *

I stood by my father's desk in the smoking-room at Innisaonar watching through the window. I was growing to love Innisaonar increasingly each year. My father always told us that a time might come when he could no longer afford to keep Innisaonar and we would have to live in nearby Thorbol Farmhouse: to leave altogether was something he could never do. My father sat behind me as I watched through the window. 'I could live here all the year,' I said to him, without turning round. 'I could not,' he replied. 'Not without the sport.' I looked towards the sea and then faced my father. 'For me that has nothing to do with it. It is the country and the light which matter.' My father seemed surprised and also pleased at what I had said. What would happen to Innisaonar when he was dead? But he was far from being an old man so why should he bother to think of such things yet? He wanted time to come to a standstill and for none of us to grow any older than we were. 'I pray to God that I will not live to be aged and decrepit and unable to do as I wish.' How many times had he said that to us all? To think of him not having the strength to walk on the hill was unimaginable. To see him with grey hair and a wrinkled face was out of the question. Youth had never left him. It was not for nothing that he was known as 'Boy'. I had offered to work for him and it was a secret moment of which no one else knew. But still he failed to teach me about the land. He refused to begin to relinquish the closed world which he had built and his own position. The magic of his youth had to be held unharmèd and the relentless years disregarded. I left him still sitting at his desk with the scent of the pine-panelled walls hanging in the air.

My father did not mind our living in London as long as he considered that we were doing something worth-while. He would have preferred us to stay at home but he never acted by force. I went to live in a respectable boarding-house, to share a room with a cousin named Flora. The landlady sat at her desk half-way up the stairs to see at what hour we came home at night. My father approved of the arrangement and thought it to be safe. I worked a half-day in an office in order to earn money to pay for the hire of a piano. The practising rooms were above an old music shop in Bond Street and the pianos were out-of-tune. I went every week to Hampstead to have lessons with a famous pianist whose other pupils were far above my standard. He was an old man and he terrified me. My hands shook as I stumbled through a Bach prelude while he sang a nursery rhyme in time. I also had lessons in harmony with a Mrs. Hubicki in Maida Vale.

Every evening Flora went out with a young man whom one day she was obviously going to marry. I sat in our room struggling with my harmony. I could not conquer chord progression. It seemed one had to be a mathematician. I rarely went out in the evening. No one asked me and I was not lonely. I had a gramophone in the room and each night I listened to Dietrich Fischer-Dieskau sing the *Winterreise*. I had heard him at the Edinburgh Festival which I had been to with Anthea the previous year. It had been a morning recital and his voice penetrated my brain as no music had done before. Now, night after night, I listened to the songs, hearing the piano illustrate each one, and experiencing the emotions of the wanderer as he treads alone on his journey, near to madness in his isolation. The music hypnotized me and I felt strangely at home with it. I grew to know every note of the piano accompaniment and every intonation of his voice. I sat wondering where each bar of music went to. I wanted to follow it to its resolution and conclusion. To capture its concrete whole. But to achieve this I knew that I must die. I often looked at the gas-fire in the room and thought how easy it would be. The beyond held a fascination for me and death now entered the scene. If I thought about it for long enough I had never had any real wish to live. But it was against my religion and I had no one to discuss these things with, so I kept them to myself.

At week-ends I always went home, and there was my father waiting for me, so that I could fling my arms around him and feel the back of his neck and his soft and perfectly cut hair which smelled of violets. At dinner he asked me questions as to whether I had eaten enough or slept enough and if I had had many late nights. He had grown to like the idea of my studying music and he often leaned through the window of our little sitting-room to listen to me practise the piano. He also liked to think that I led a gay life in London. I let him keep that illusion. We could not talk of death.

*   *   *

It was in the spring that Martin was sent to stay with us at Fields. There was a dance to be held in a large country house and the hostess asked if we would invite two of her guests, one of whom was Martin, for the week-end. Margaret and I knew that Martin had written a book about his life in a German prison-camp during the war, so therefore he must be much older than us. We took out the book from the bookshelves in the drawing-room and searched through the pages until we came to a photograph of his portrait, painted by a fellow prisoner. The portrait was in profile. A young, thin and mournful face with a strong nose and chin. It was a striking portrait but Margaret and I glanced at each other quickly; he had a drooping moustache. That would not do for us. I studied his face over and over again before he arrived to stay. The picture intrigued me as also did his book. To have been held hostage by the Germans sounded to me extremely romantic and I had met the painter of the portrait when I was eleven years old. That had been just after the war and I had fallen in love with him because he had the look of a hunted hare and he was the only person who ever liked my mice. He had preferred to watch them quietly, with me by his side, rather than to be in the company of the other grown-ups. He, too, had been held hostage. Martin must know him very well.

I waited anxiously for the day when Martin would arrive. He was an older man and surely my father would not banish him to our little sitting-room as though he were a child? The day came and the other man arrived punctually by train. He, too, was older than Margaret and me. I did not pay much attention to him. I waited for Martin. We sat through the dinner-party before the dance and still he did not come. At last I heard the noise of wheels on gravel and someone walk in through the door and straight up the stairs. Martin had arrived and he went directly to Anthea's room where she was lying in bed recovering from an illness. My father was furious at his behaviour. We wondered why he went to Anthea's bedroom? And how did he know the way? He never gave any explanation. While he was eating his dinner, I went to my room and made myself as pretty as I could. My father had already turned against Martin and I had not yet met him. But in my mind he symbolized the freedom for which I craved. I sensed that it was no ordinary occasion and I trembled as I walked down the stairs. I stopped and listened. I thought I heard a roaring in the air, but no, only the murmuring of voices coming from the drawing-room. I entered the room. Margaret had already joined the gathering. Martin stood under a lamp. I recognized him at once from his portrait. But now he was clean-shaven. My father abruptly introduced us. We shook hands and I noticed his brilliant blue eyes and his insouciant smile. I drove to the dance with my father and spent much of the time with him. I did dance with Martin but we did not talk very much. On the way home I sat next to him and he put his hand out to hold mine. And I defied my father and fell in love with Martin.

After I had gone to bed I longed to creep down the stairs to Martin's room and stand in my night-dress beside his bed. The moon was bright to show him that I had come. And we would embrace silently because he knew without being told that he had been sent to save me from my bondage. I stood outside my door but I dared not walk down the stairs. My father would hear them creaking and know of my betrayal of him.

The next day we sat outside in the warm spring sun. Daffodils were massed and shone down the long straight drive. Martin took off his jacket, rolled up his shirt sleeves, opened the neck of his shirt and stretched out his long legs. My father did not like that, he had not asked permission to take off his jacket. Martin took it for granted that he would sit in the drawing-room. My father asked him to leave and to join Margaret and me in our little sitting-room. I felt ashamed. I took him for a walk down a farm track. Martin showed me how he could tread on the electric wire fence without getting a shock. Everything he did was as though he were playing a game. He told me how during the last year he had rescued a friend of his from the Foreign Legion in North Africa. It had been a difficult and a dangerous adventure and he had written a book about it. We leaned against a haystack in the sun and I watched Martin. There was a vagueness about him which could be taken for boredom, but he seemed interested in everything. And then he touched my hair and caressed me as though he were playing with a little child or animal. He excited and fascinated me. I had never met anyone like him before.

It was time for him to leave. We walked back to the house and we did not speak. But I was determined that we would play our serious game again.

My opportunity to do so came very soon. I was invited to bring a partner to a ball which was to be held in the

Chelsea Royal Hospital. I wrote and asked Martin if he would like to come. He accepted and asked me for a meal in his flat which he called his 'eyrie' before the dance. Anthea questioned me as to whom I was going to take. When I told her she leaned back on the sofa. 'I will not tell your father,' she said. She, too, had been held by Martin's charm and sympathised with me. She knew, though, that my father's dislike of him had been so great that he might have forbidden me to see Martin again. He would have considered it dangerous. But my father knew without being told what was going to happen. A short while after Martin had been to stay he had told Anthea sadly that he knew I was going to marry someone whom he could never approve of, but that he would not stop me from doing what I wished.

The evening of the ball arrived and I shook with excitement at the thought of seeing Martin again. I drove in a taxi to the street where he lived. The door of the house was open. The paint was cracked and peeling. I walked straight through the door and up the stairs to the top of the house. There were flights and flights of green linoleum stairs. At the top of the house there was a bright pink door. Martin's name was written on the door in red letters. I knocked. I tried to look serene. Then the door opened and Martin stood there. I walked into his room and this is what I saw:

It was a long room with a high glass ceiling. One wall was papered green, dotted with harps. Another was brown, patterned with bees. The third was black, covered with wreaths. A grand piano stood at the end of the room. I stood beside a painted chest. It was a Spanish chest and it was covered in dust. A great many bottles had been placed on it. Empty bottles and bottles half-filled with wine. There was a large picture hanging above the chest. It was a picture full of birds and in the distance, a lake.

There were many different kinds of birds, all congregating unnaturally together. White birds of all sizes and peacocks and a hen in a basket which hung from the wall in their barn. It was a Dutch picture and Martin had told me that he was half-Dutch. There were old yellow curtains at the windows. They did not fit the windows. On the floor there was a piece of carpet. The boards it tried to cover were thick with dust. There were two armchairs. The linen covers of the chairs were dirty. Between the chairs there was a glass table. The table was strewn with papers and small boxes and objects. There was a brass pig which was an ink-stand, a match-box case with DRAWING ROOM written on the top, and a white china pear. Things lay everywhere. Books and pencils and papers. Everything was covered in dust and everything was old and worn. There were paper cut-outs pasted on the door – scraps of Roman emperors which were peeling at the corners. It was hot in the room. There was a musty smell of eucalyptus and mimosa. The room was hidden. It was pretty and beautiful. I had never seen such a room before.

Martin cooked me an omelette and we drank some wine. I felt shy in his presence and of being in an environment so totally different from any I had known. Martin seemed perfectly at ease and left me for a moment to change his clothes. He returned wearing a dinner-jacket. It was not until we drove up to the Chelsea Royal Hospital did I dare to tell him that the Queen was going to be there. Martin told the taxi driver to return to where he lived and I waited for him while he went in search of a white tie and tails. Eventually he reappeared in the correct clothes and although they were slightly creased and grubby he took on the air of an indefatigable and beautiful adventurer.

It was a warm night in June and Wren's building was

flood-lit against the blue-black summer sky. Half-way through the night Martin disappeared. I searched for him amongst the crowds but he was nowhere to be found. I started to panic. The marquee was full of unfamiliar faces. I had no line of communication with anyone. I stood rigid against a pillar. I had no shadow and I was alone like a Giacometti. The people in the marquee were alive. Their movements were fluid with life as they danced. I was dead as though I were carved out of wood. After a long time Martin suddenly appeared again. He was totally unconcerned because he thought I would know many people. He had been to visit another party which was being held in London that night. I did not tell him of my terror.

We walked into the gardens. Moths fluttered around the lights. We went to the tennis-courts where it was dark and quiet. I told Martin how troubled I was and how I thirsted to reach the Absolute, and that the only way I could conceive of achieving it was through suicide. I had no one else to tell or who could speak my language except for Martin. He listened carefully and half-understood but he did not realize how serious I was and thought I was going through a youthful romantic phase. And he lifted up my face and kissed me under the magnitude of the stars and the sky in the tennis-courts of the Chelsea Royal Hospital. Then we ran together over the lawns and up mown banks, with me tripping over my dress, its scarlet sash flying out behind, back to the lights and the music and the end of the ball.

Martin returned me to where I lived. 'Let me kiss you over the threshold,' he said, before I closed the door.

Every evening I sat in the boarding-house waiting for the telephone to ring. Every evening Flora went out with her young man and I continued to work on my harmony and listen to the *Winterreise* and hope for Martin to contact me as he had promised to do. After some weeks he telephoned and asked me to go with him to a party.

The party began late at night and it was held in an artist's house in Chelsea. The door of the house was left wide open and the rooms were crowded with people I had never seen before. I met a philosopher and a writer and a painter. They were so very different from the young men who had attended the dances I had previously been to. I thought that I had at last found a world where I wanted to be. Once again Martin disappeared and I found myself alone amongst all these strangers who were in various stages of drunkenness. Once again I was terribly afraid. An older man came up to me and said that Martin had asked him to take care of me. He had had to leave the party in order to discuss with a girl whether or not he was going to marry her. They had broken off their love affair a few weeks before but she had arrived at the party unexpectedly and he had to talk with her in privacy. They had gone to the Chelsea Embankment for a final discussion. I felt bewildered and shaken and very near to tears.

'Let me take you home,' the man said.

'No, I shall wait for Martin to return,' I insisted.

'You little fool, don't you realize it's a matter of life or death?' the man replied, letting me know how crucial the situation was. I did not answer and he walked away. In despair I waited for Martin, determined to see it through. Were all my dreams to be shattered? Martin did return as I felt sure he would, breathless and seemingly untroubled at the end of his latest affair. I wanted him to keep me safe and like a child I clung to him, tired and frightened. The dawn broke.

'It's time to go home,' Martin said. I searched for my bag in the garden where I had laid it down. I searched for it in the house. It was nowhere to be found. An intruder had stolen it. I could not get into the boarding-house. My key was gone.

'You must come with me,' Martin said. And I found myself climbing the flights of green linoleum stairs to his flat at the top of the house where he lived. I lay down beside him on his bed in my white starched petticoat, and he put his arms around me as though I were a doll, and we slept.

In the morning I looked at Martin's bedroom. The wall-paper was pale blue. The paper had a pattern of small white squiggles which looked like drawings of breasts and navels. But it was just an ordinary white pattern on blue paper. Photographs of girls were pinned on the walls. The bed was French Empire and very short in length. On a table beside the bed there was an old bowler hat. The hat was full of pennies for the telephone-meter. At the window there was a sooty net curtain. Outside on the window-ledge there was a geranium in a pot. The plant was not growing well. It was not a suitable place for a plant to grow, perched on a window-ledge high up, outside an old building in London. It received only dust and shade. The window was tightly shut and the panes were cloudy. A waft of dried flowers came faintly from the studio. My body shivered. I felt life, not abstraction.

Then, on a bright summer morning, I crept guiltily back to my boarding-house.

*   *   *

I spent the late summer days at Innisaonar dreaming of Martin and of the new world I had glimpsed through him. I walked alone on the hill wondering what Martin would think of it if he ever came to Innisaonar. But what was I now going to do with my father? My beloved father. I was still bound to him. I loved Innisaonar more intensely than ever before. My father was continually telling us to make the most of our life at home while we still had it. He seemed to feel that the time was drawing near when he might lose us at any moment. He did not want any changes. He feared my growing independence. He feared his own growing older. He denied its happening. Eternal childhood and eternal youth would reign over Innisaonar. Its magic would hold me for him in the image of my mother and of his only son. And its magic would hold himself for always as the commanding, just and fairest 'Boy'.

It was in October that I had my twenty-first birthday. Margaret had had a dance given for her at Fields when she was twenty-one but I did not want a dance. I had planned a mysterious party with my father. Margaret could not be there because she was in London learning to be a florist. William could not be there because he had been given a day's stalking forty miles away.

It was a clear autumn morning with the sun shining in a bright blue sky and I came down to breakfast and embraced my father with more violence in my heart than I had ever done. And there in front of me was my gift from him. Small leather boxes were piled on the table and in each box there was a jewel. Pearls and diamonds, crystals and emeralds, torquoise, opals, sapphires and jade. Earrings, necklaces, bracelets and rings. They had belonged to my mother. I hung the necklaces round my neck, the bracelets round my wrists and put the rings on my fingers. I stood in front of my father dressed as my young mother. I was overjoyed with all my jewels and I ran round the house showing myself off. And my father smiled when he saw me. And then he handed me an envelope and inside I found a ticket and written on it was the number of a tape-recorder he was to give me, which was something I had wanted for long but my father had regarded them as 'useless toys'. Now he had given me what I wished. Also in the envelope were twenty-five pound notes to buy whatever I liked.

The party I had planned was to be held in a small derelict croft which lies in the hills, inaccessible except from the stony track which leads past the grave. In the distance Loch Tarvie can be seen, black and deep; above the loch, Ben Tarvie with its rock face looking like the Sphinx. I arranged the party down to the smallest detail. With Louisa, who was now eight years old, we carried candles and baskets of unharmed roses. They were just the heads of red roses which we had picked from the garden. With great labour we took them the long way to the croft. We hung blue curtains at the window to darken the tiny room and placed the candles in the empty whisky bottles which the Irish hill drainers who had last stayed in the croft had left behind. We spread rugs on the floor and scattered the rose heads over them. We lit a fire in the grate and piled it with peat, and the room looked secret and alive. It was the fulfilment of a dream which I had planned for months. The food was brought to the croft by Gunn in the Land-Rover and we laid it between the rose heads. My birthday cake was made of peaches and cream and there were crackers and the old H.M.V. gramophone. When everything was ready we waited for Anthea and my father to arrive. Maybe they came reluctantly, thinking that it was just one of my ideas. But when the kettle was put on the fire to make the tea my father started to enjoy himself. His labrador dog stretched herself out on the floor and the feast began. Afterwards I played Chopin waltzes and the *Écossaises* on the gramophone and to please my father, Binnie Hale singing 'As Time Goes By'. He sat outside on the grass, wearing a paper hat from a cracker. A lock of hair fell over his face, and made him look like a youth. I knew that my father enjoyed my party. It was beautiful. I stayed by myself after they had all left and sat there until the fire went down. As I left the croft that evening I turned to look at it in the darkening October light. Smoke was still coming from the chimney and I knew with bitterness that it would never happen again.

*   *   *

Immediately I returned to London I wondered what to buy with my twenty-five pounds. On the first day, as I left the music shop in Bond Street after practising the piano, I stopped at an art gallery to look at a picture which caught my eye. It was a small water-colour by Wilson Steer. It was of a river and trees and it was painted all in blue. It had the still and shadowy quality which was now increasingly embracing me and pulling me to a world of the beyond. I could not tell whether the picture had been painted in the dawn or the dusk, but to me it was the concrete illustration of my thought and the place where I so much wished to reach. No living thing except the trees was shown. I stood for a long time listening to the silence of the picture amongst the noise of the traffic, and that strange place in my mind beckoned me towards it in order that I might lose myself. I went into the gallery and asked how much the picture cost. The man told me it was fifty pounds. All day long and throughout the evening the picture haunted me. I returned the next day and the next to get its impression again. I knew that I had to have it.

During the months at Innisaonar I had waited for the time when I could see Martin again. I decided I would ask his advice about the picture. It took great courage on my part to telephone him and when at last I did, he asked me to his flat. On the telephone I heard voices in the distance and I imagined his room to be full of people. I got myself ready to go but I was so afraid of facing a crowd that I could not leave my room. After two hours Martin rang up and asked what had happened to me. I told him that I thought he was having a party but he said there had been no one. I met him in a café in the street where he lived. He was sitting looking rather cross, wearing a high-necked jersey, and his thick hair was tousled. I asked him about the Wilson Steer water-colour. He said he thought it was a Bond Street price but that if I liked it enough I should buy it. I returned to the boarding-house in a euphoric state of mind. Martin had confirmed the justification of buying my Wilson Steer. The next day I went to the art gallery and they agreed to let me pay the extra twenty-five pounds in three instalments. I carried the picture down Bond Street amazed at what I had. I showed it to Flora. She did not understand. I took it home with me. I could hardly wait to show my father what I had bought with his present. I tore off the brown paper in the drawing-room and put the picture in front of my father and Anthea. 'Mm,' they said, and expressed no other opinion or appreciation. My father could not see its beauty nor feel its magical power. He did not know of the land where I felt compelled to go. I took the picture to my room and I treasured it.

Flora and I were tired of the restrictions of the boarding-house and of sharing the same room. We wanted to move into a flat of our own where we could lead a more independent life. We found a furnished flat in a basement in Draycott Avenue where the rent was not too high. It was dark and dingy and was the first we looked at, but in our eyes it meant freedom and we were determined to get it. Flora got permission from her parents. My father did not like the idea but he reluctantly agreed to come and see it. I do not think that my father had ever been in that part of London before. On his visits he walked down Bond Street and Jermyn Street, through Mayfair and up beside Green Park to Clarges Street. The owner and landlady of the flat showed my father round. He inspected everything critically and said nothing. He would not commit himself. He did not give a definite 'No', neither would he say 'Yes'.

At home for the week-end Margaret and I rebelled together at the crippling restrictions which were being imposed more and more on us. I decided to take things into my own hands. Both Flora and the landlady were waiting for an agreement. When my father was out I dared to go into the drawing-room and use the telephone. I telephoned the landlady of the basement flat and told her we would definitely take it, and immediately. She replied that she had thought my father had disapproved of the flat so much that she had already let it to someone else. I put down the receiver with resentment mounting inside me. For the first time in my life I realized that I wanted my father to die. I actually willed his death for my own freedom. A furious and a blinding rage tore through me and I lay on the floor and screamed and screamed.

I met my father in the drive returning from a walk. I told him what had happened and I shouted at him. 'I am sorry, dear,' he said. I knew that he meant it but he did not suggest anything else. He was refusing to allow me to run into what he thought might be any kind of danger. A huge late October sun glowed in the sky. I had wanted my father to die. In the damp autumn air of the Cotswolds, which was not our home-land, we drew close together.

The following week I was lying in bed in the boarding-house having finished my harmony for the evening and I had just turned out the light when in the darkness I saw before me as though on a huge cinema screen, a picture of my father. He was sitting on the garden wall smiling to me and swinging his legs as he always did like a young man. The colours of the picture were so brilliant that my eyes could not stand it. I closed them and when I opened them again the picture was still there, shining with a purity I had never seen before. At last the picture faded and in its place with the same supernatural colours there came the face of Jesus Christ framed in a rose-window. It stayed for I do not know how long and then it too faded. And in awe I wondered and tried to put it from my mind, but I could not do so.

The next week-end I went home as usual. William was now living in the boarding-house. He had left the army and my father had arranged for him to work in a solicitor's office. He was not happy. The work did not suit him. He spent nearly all the evenings in our room looking for companionship. We went home together. It was an un-eventful week-end at the beginning of November. One evening my father, Anthea, Margaret and myself were sitting in the drawing-room. My father suddenly said, waving his hand towards us: 'If anything happens to me I leave it to you to look after Gunn and the others at Innisaonar.' I believe that his remark about death passed almost unnoticed, so distant and impossible it seemed, but I know it struck me as being right in place and time.

William had now an old car which he drove around the country but he was strictly forbidden to drive it to London. Margaret was staying at home for a time and William and I were supposed to drive to the station to catch the Sunday evening train. We conspired together. We decided to go against my father's orders and drive the whole way to London and have a good dinner on the way to celebrate our disobedience. That evening we had many things to take back with us. William packed into the car his collection of antique knives and swords which he planned to hide under his bed and I had piles of long white petticoats that I always brought home to starch. We got into the car and set off into the night. 'Good-bye, Dad,' I had said from the doorway of the drawing-room. My father had sat in his chair and I had not kissed him. How could I, when I was about to betray him? I was always aware of the act of Judas. William and I ate our expensive dinner in a restaurant near Henley. We drank two bottles of wine and became hilarious. The number-plate of the car fell off with a loud clattering before we reached London and William had to tie it on with a piece of string. At last, late at night, laughing like the devil, we climbed the stairs of the boarding-house, carrying the knives and swords and petticoats.

And I was sore afraid.

*　　*　　*

It was two days later, early in the morning that Anthea telephoned me. She said that my father had had a brain haemorrhage and was lying in the Radcliffe Infirmary in Oxford. The doctors said they did not know whether he would live or die but that if he lived he would never be the same again. Anthea was staying with friends in Oxford and I told her I would come home immediately to be with Margaret and to wait. I reacted coldly, without any feeling. I went to the hairdresser. My father would wish me to look correct while I watched him fighting with death. I caught the next train home. Margaret met me at the station with Louisa and Mounette. We could not talk of our father's illness in front of Louisa so instead we spoke about her dancing-class. It was an agonizing drive. And then Margaret took me to our little sitting-room and told me all. She said that it had been a beautiful autumn day and our father had returned from an afternoon's shooting looking happy and saying how well he felt. It was just before tea and as Margaret was going to the dining-room she heard someone coughing in the cloakroom. There she found our father lying on the floor which was covered with his blood. Our father who had always been independent was now lying helpless on the floor. 'Don't touch me,' he managed to say. No one was to see him at a disadvantage. His suffering did not last long. He lost consciousness in the ambulance on the way to Oxford. Anthea went with him. It was November the fifth, Guy Fawkes night, and rockets were shooting towards the sky as if to celebrate the falling of a star. Bonfires were lit all over the countryside and the November night was on fire.

My dearest, dearest Margaret. How could she have borne it? But she had been present. She had discovered our father and had lived through it. It was real to her. It was not to me. I cursed myself for not being there at the right time. We spent the evening in the drawing-room listening to a Beethoven piano concerto on the wireless and waiting for the telephone to ring. Our father's labrador dog wandered round the house. She would not settle in her basket. Meals were something to be got through. All we wanted to talk about was our father but we knew that Owen and Mrs. Jones had their ears to the keyhole of the door. We either kept silent or spoke about ordinary things.

What should we pray for? To think of our father as an imbecile cripple was unthinkable. He, my fair hero. 'Lord have mercy on him,' I could not pray. I waited and wanted him to die as I felt he wished to do. He was fifty years old and he would have fought against old age.

Anthea returned from Oxford. Our father's unconsciousness was so deep that the doctors told Anthea to go

home and wait. For three long days we waited; facing
limbo or death. Anthea and Margaret prayed. I waited
for my father to die.

On the fourth day the hospital telephoned to ask us to
come. Our father was sinking even deeper. We drove to
Oxford. We sat in a little cubicle with my father's sister
who loved her darling 'Boy'. Anthea went to be by his side.
A few minutes later she returned. Our father was dead.

I remember sitting on a bench with Margaret outside
the hospital in the sun and we said: 'He was half of us.'
Then we went to a flower-stall and bought as many
flowers as we could. I do not know why I was the one to
do it but I took the flowers to a young nurse and she held
them in her arms to take them to my father. I looked at
her sweet face which was so sad for me and I reluctantly
turned away from her to confront the hell and guilt and
unreality commonly known, to those who are left behind,
as death.

The days which followed were ones of grotesque activity
instead of peace. We became like secretaries, answering the
telephone, writing letters and making arrangements. Owen
and Mrs. Jones and Jamesina and Rayne, the Scottish
housemaids, avoided our eyes and spent the time whisper-
ing in the kitchen. Louisa was determined not to be left
out and so she was included. I felt sorry for Mounette
alone in the nursery with my black cat, Puss. William
returned, shocked and broken. Esmond, assuming a role
as head of the family, came back for the first time in years.
I tried to understand his previous unhappiness and this
now protective feeling towards his mother. But to see him
sitting on the sofa in the drawing-room, greatly discom-
forted me.

My father had never wished for a large funeral. He
always said that he wanted to disappear without any
ostentation. Anthea said that death needed ceremony. A

public funeral was organized. Why was he not to be buried at Innisaonar on the hill? The day before the funeral Margaret and I went to the village church at Fields and arranged flowers in vases on the altar. While we were doing so we heard the grave-diggers digging the hole in the ground, making a dull thudding noise with their pick-axes. Grave-diggers digging a grave for my father? How could that be possible? I envied Anthea and Margaret. They were able to show grief with their tears and their sorrow. I was like a figure of stone. No emotion entered me.

And then it was about to happen. The committing of my father's body to the earth. We went to the church in the middle of a golden November day. In the unreality of of the moment I could see no faces. Only a mass of people crowding into the church all dressed in black. And I heard the words: 'The Lord gave, and the Lord hath taken away.' How could it be so? The vicar had started the service without us. My father would be furious at our unpunctuality. Beside me in front of the altar was my father's coffin, draped in the Union Jack. How could my father's body be lying there? And near to the coffin was my cousin dressed in the brightly coloured uniform of the Life Guards. He stood so rigidly. As the service progressed I gazed at the Union Jack. Its colours melted together in front of my eyes. Everything was a haze around me. I heard the music and hymns and the service for the burial of the dead but I did not join in. And then came these words:

'I Esdras saw upon the Mount Sion a great people whom I could not number, and they all praised the Lord with songs. And in the midst of them there was a young man of a high stature, taller than all the rest, and upon every one of their heads he set crowns, and was more exalted; which I marvelled at greatly. So I asked the angel, and said, Sir, what are these? He answered and said unto me, These be they that have put off the mortal clothing, and put on the immortal, and have confessed the name of God: now are they crowned, and receive palms. Then said I unto the angel, What young person is it that crowneth them, and giveth palms in their hands? So he answered and said unto me, It is the Son of God, whom they have confessed in the world. Then began I greatly to commend them that stood so stiffly for the name of the Lord. Then the angel said unto me, Go thy way, and tell my people what manner of things, and how great wonders of the Lord thy God thou hast seen.'

As the service drew to a close, Gunn and other men from Innisaonar appeared and lifted my father gently on their shoulders. What pain there was in their strong faces. As they carried my father's coffin out of the church, Anthea and Louisa followed them and then my father's sister and after her Margaret and myself and last of all, Esmond and William. I could see nothing except for the Union Jack and I began to run. Margaret put out her hand and held me back. And beneath a yew tree my father was lowered into his grave as the Last Post was sounded. I do not know how long I stood staring into the deep deep grave. But suddenly I realized I was all alone and stepped back over the rough grass. I walked past throngs of people, and returned to the car where my father's black labrador dog lay. When we reached Fields we went to the stable yard and shook hands with those who had come from Innisaonar. As I took Gunn's hand our eyes met and it was as though we were searching for something between us. Three weeks ago my father, he and I, had all taken part in my birthday in the hills at home. The one and only tear that I could shed rolled down my face.

A neighbour from Scotland was staying to be with Anthea and we all gathered into the drawing-room. I sat on the floor, hiding behind my father's chair, and played

G   97

snakes and ladders with Louisa. I could not see the board or read what the dice said.

And then I had to rise and go again. To return to my father's grave before it grew dark. Multitudes of flowers lay there and I picked my way between them to reach him once more. I bent to collect a card from a wreath. I picked it at random. It was from the people at Innisaonar, Skelbo, Thorbol and Coul. 'With treasured memories of our beloved Colonel', it read. And then I lived again in detail every part of the day. The ceremonious day. And when I got back I sat in my room like a stone, and there was no letting go even when darkness came over me.

*   *   *

William returned to the boarding-house. Esmond went away. He eventually emigrated to Australia, where he found happiness. The neighbour from Scotland left and Anthea retired to bed suffering from exhaustion. Louisa was only allowed in her room at certain hours. She sat on a chair, her feet kicking against it and annoying Anthea. Margaret and I took it in turns to stay with Anthea in her bedroom. She did not want to be left alone. The weather was growing cold and I lay on the floor in her room wrapped in an eiderdown, listening to Scarlatti on the wireless and answering letters.

I expected to see my father at any moment. He would walk round the corner and embrace me or give me an order. His stick still stood in the corner of the cloakroom and his hat hung on a hook. It smelled of his violet hair-oil, and I would creep into the cloakroom every day and take it from its peg and smell it, inhaling its scent as deeply as I could, thus finding him again. But his chair in the drawing-room remained empty and a bowl of violets stood on the table beside it. I drank a whole bottle of my father's port. I hoped it would release some feeling inside me. It had no effect. I remained like a pillar of stone. I tried in vain to pray but my words came out meaningless.

The day came when Anthea had to attend a meeting of my father's executors in London. I accompanied her. My father had left no detailed will. He had said that he had written what he wished to be carried out on his death in a little black book. The house was turned upside down in search of the little black book. It was never found either at Innisaonar or Fields. Perhaps it had never existed. Had not my father told us that it was for us to provide for the people at Innisaonar? His wish was never met.

I waited on the platform at Paddington for Anthea to return. Somehow we missed each other and when I at last found her she was in a state of desperation. She visualized a life of loss and insecurity. When we arrived at Fields she collapsed. Margaret and I became alarmed and telephoned the doctor. That night I stayed with her beside her bed and as she held my hand in her agony she let out a confession: 'And now,' she said, 'all I have to live for is Louisa.' In the darkness I could feel the hot sweat of the palm of her hand and the hard metal of her rings, and I turned icy cold.

Margaret looked strained and tired. It was time for her to have a break and she went to London for the day. We agreed to take it in turns to leave Anthea. Instead of Fields being a home it had become a hell. I was so badly in need of comfort that I wrote to Martin and asked if I could come and see him. I received no reply.

When Margaret returned I went to London all dressed in black. We were in mourning for our father. It was the time of the Hungarian Revolution. I pretended that I was in mourning for the Hungarians and not for my father because he was not dead for me. There was no light around me and the branches of the trees appeared to me to be dripping with blood. I saw their bark dripping tears of blood.

I telephoned Martin when I reached London and he asked me to his flat. He had not answered my letter because he had been away on the Hungarian border giving aid to the refugees. I sat all the evening in his studio where I so wished to be. I asked to stay the night with him and sinned against my father for the first time in my life.

I do not remember the leaving very well. Everything looked grey and shadowy. I walked down the street and saw the writing on the sign which hung next door to the house where Martin lived. 'Thirteenth Church of Christ Scientist London', it said. I caught a bus to Park Lane and sat in a café meaning to catch the next train back to Fields. Suddenly the café became absolutely still and silent like a picture. The world of the beyond, the world of my Wilson Steer water-colour, was pulling me towards it with a force far stronger than myself. I began to sweat and tremble. I knew that I must go to the boarding-house to the empty room and turn on the gas-fire as I had often longed to do. Then I would at last reach the peace at the centre of the vortex through death. When I got to South Kensington my reason told me that I had a duty towards God, and also to my father. I telephoned Martin from the tube station and he told me to come to him at once. He sat me in a chair and wrapped a rug around me. I half lost consciousness and all I saw was the reflection of a sea-gull above the glass ceiling, its image floating on the top of a glass table in front of me. It swooped and circled in the sky and I watched the bird until Martin put me into his bed. I stayed there for three nights and three days, half-knowing what had happened and half not knowing. During the day Martin wrote his book in the studio. I heard the keys of the typewriter clicking through the door. He told me that he was writing a biography of a military man. In the evenings he played his gramophone to arouse me. He played Mozart's E flat Litany over and over again. He came into the bedroom to see me many times. Each time he came he put his hand against my face. I felt it rough against my skin. I buried my face in his hand. I prayed to God to fill me wholly so I could rise and go again but my prayer was not answered. My sin was too great. On the fourth day I left and returned to Fields. I sent my soul away. Only my body, my empty body could be persuaded to go back to the hell and the truth.

Once again I found myself in Anthea's bedroom but this time I could no longer help her. As with Margaret, the strain had become too much. I told Anthea that all I wished for was to die by suicide. The local doctor came. He asked me if it was the publicity I wanted. I laughed and laughed. 'Poor little man,' I thought. I went into the cloakroom and leaned against my father's stick and smelled that scent of violets and laughed like a demon over the place where he had lain. I was put to bed with sleeping medicine. The next day Owen Jones drove Anthea, Margaret and myself to London to stay the night at Claridge's, where I was to see the neurologist who had followed me through my life. We were shown into a suite which had thick pile carpets and mirrors everywhere. Steam heat rose from the floors. And on a table in the middle of the suite was a large vase of chrysanthemums. They were huge bronze blooms, unreal and funereal and underneath was a neat little card from the manager expressing his sympathy. My father had been a regular visitor to Claridge's. I acted like a film star. I had to play my part. Instead of a black dress, I changed into a grey one with a swirling skirt. Anthea went downstairs and I heard her tell Margaret that on no account was she to let me out. Margaret, my own sister, had become my gaoler. The suite, with its flashy mirrors, had become a prison. Even Martin, who had rescued a friend from the Foreign Legion, would not be able to get me out of here. What were they doing to me? Fury mounted inside me but I kept up my act. We had dinner in the dining-room and afterwards the neurologist arrived. He sat drinking crème de menthe with Anthea in an alcove. How smooth and smart he was. I was sent to the suite where he shortly joined me. I offered him cigarettes from my father's gold cigarette case and sat poised in a chair answering his questions with the polite evasiveness of an actress being interviewed about her private life.

As we went to bed I raised my arms and clenched my fists and I attacked Anthea. I went for her with my heart raging against her.

I was taken to see a psychiatrist who wanted to shut me up in his clinic and give me electric shock treatments and suggested other cures which were so offensive to me that I refused to co-operate. The psychiatrist tried to hold me but I knew that electric shock treatment would take me away from my interior world, from my father and the tension which was the root of my existence. So I fled from the psychiatrist and then they left me alone. Martin found me a room in the Cromwell Road which was owned by a lady who made costumes for the ballet. There Puss, my old black cat, pining for the country, died. There I, pining for my father, took an overdose of sleeping pills but they saved me.

Anthea and my father's executors decided to sell both Innisaonar and Fields. Anthea could not bear the thought of either without my father. She bought a house in London for herself and Louisa and Mounette, and a little house in the country where we could come and visit. Margaret, William and I who had always been kept as children and protected from the outside world suddenly found ourselves without a home at all. We were shocked and unprepared for life and all of us lost our way. I wanted to go home to my father, so I persuaded them not to sell the whole of Innisaonar and they reluctantly allowed me Skelbo House on the estate.

*　　*　　*

And then there was the memorial service for our father. It was held in Dornoch Cathredal, six miles from Innisaonar. It was a dark winter day with snow-flakes falling. We stood in the starkly pure interior of the little sandstone cathedral. The words and hymns of the funeral service were repeated. Once again I saw no faces, only a crowd of people dressed in sombre clothes. As I watched the snow-flakes melting on my coat, I felt closer to my father than I had done since his death. I still shed no tears because I knew it was impossible for me ever truly to be betrothed to any man save him.

And I prayed for our father and for ourselves and for the forgiveness of our sins.

PART 3

And you, my father, there on the sad height,
Curse, bless, me now with your fierce tears, I pray.
Do not go gentle into that good night.
Rage, rage against the dying of the light.
                    Dylan Thomas

Skelbo is a house and a farm and a ruined castle. Its name in Norse means 'place of shells'. The house stands high on a hill overlooking the farm, the sea loch and the sea with its wild beaches. Skelbo is in the past, present and future. I hope that it may enter my future and be in my present once more because each part of it has its own meaning for me. I am afraid, too afraid of the empty spaces to go there again but with all my strength I will not allow it to become my past because where would I find again what I might leave behind?

*   *   *

When William and I were fourteen years old there came an early morning when we went from Innisaonar. All the doors had been locked for the previous night so we left by the kitchen window, making as little noise as possible. It was forbidden and it was an adventure. We knew that gypsies were living in the ruins of Skelbo Castle. We had seen them arrive, making their way along the route from Caithness. An old caravan drawn by a thin horse with several ponies and lurcher dogs following behind them. And then there were the parents with their children.

That morning we bicycled along the small road round the tidal Loch Fleit until we reached the castle ruins. We walked up the field where they stand on their high mount and then crawled on our stomachs to the top to look through the hole in the walls which are made of crumbling grey stone and the mortar of sand and of mussel shells.

The caravan stood in the hollow of the ruins with its back against the seventeenth-century house which has now fallen apart. It was a beautiful caravan; faded pink and green, its shafts lying in the long grass and nettles. We kept very quiet so as not to disturb the gypsies. We watched them waking, yawning, stretching their arms in the sun, chattering and shouting and lighting their fire. The lurcher dogs, their tails between their legs, sniffed around the tethered ponies.

Afterwards I learned that the family's name was Wandlen, a well-known gypsy name in the Orkneys and Caithness. They stayed for some years. The man worked on the farm and having no means to tell the time, would keep on working until dusk. He was a dark man with a handsome face. The farm people said: 'He has tinker's ways but is good enough...' My father liked him and always told him the time although it did not seem to mean very much to him.

We watched them that morning for a long while and then returned. We looked back at the great clump of trees at the top of another hill behind the castle. Just the point of a turret could be seen but few would have guessed that a house stood there. 'That is where I shall live one day,' I said to William. He made no comment. The curlews had begun.

*   *   *

Skelbo House has had a varied history. It was built in 1866 by a Duke of Sutherland. He had built it as a small picnic house, a folly, where the shooting parties from Dunrobin Castle could perhaps stay for a night or two. Barry, the great Victorian architect, had built massively on to Dunrobin for the Duke of Sutherland and it was almost certainly he who drew the sketches for Skelbo House although it was not built so elegantly as he intended.

At the time of the death of my father, nearly a hundred years later, an old lady was living in Skelbo House. She had lived there for forty years and she loved it with her whole heart. She had been married to the tenant farmer when my grandfather bought the estate. Long ago when the farmer was going to a sheep sale in his pony and trap he had left his little son alone with a paraffin lamp beside his bed in the dark early morning. The child knocked the lamp over. The bed caught fire and the child was burnt to death. Things went slowly down hill for the farmer and his family. When their days had been good they had employed a coachman, a cook and a maid. The farmer got into debt and finally he committed suicide by drinking cyanide in the great steading where he was found dead. His widow was allowed by my grandfather to remain in the house. She was a gentle lady whom one only met at garden fêtes and I would sell her bunches of flowers from behind the stalls and we talked with pleasure about her many cats. She had nineteen in all. Her life must have been hard and lonely but she always appeared serene and happy and unafraid. She never locked a door at night. She had a goodness and a faith undisturbed by the outside world. Not long after my father died she had a heart attack and was found dead by a woman on the farm, beside the old iron range in the kitchen.

*　　*　　*

Skelbo House is very difficult to find. I write instructions: Drive along the sea loch road until you reach the castle. Turn right on to the rough farm track and drive over the two bridges across the burn. The house and garden are surrounded by a grey stone wall. At that time no house could be seen until one was at the door. 'Do you think you'll be all right here?' Anthea asked. I did not reply. A pink sandstone house with two round pointed turrets stood before me. The turrets had iron decorations of thistles and little flags with fleur-de-lis. The windows copied a Scottish baronial style with their small window panes set deeply into the walls to keep out the weather and untoward attackers. Their woodwork was painted a dark green, peeling and rotting away. The small gables had stone balls on their tops. The front gable and porch had cut-stone crow-steps and behind them was the grey slated roof. The house looked like a ghost, uninviting, as though it had a pile of secrets hidden in it. If it had not been for its small size it could have been described as being extremely ugly. As it was, it had a curious charm in its derelict way, with the beech trees tapping on the window panes. Trees were everywhere. I could hardly see the house for the old sycamores, beeches, pines, hollies, ivy and yew. The house appeared as an illusion amongst the mass of tree trunks and foliage.

The inside of the house was bare of furniture except for a rocking-horse in one of the upstair rooms. Many of the floors were made of rough Caithness flagstones. The rooms in the turrets were small, almost an octagonal shape, and the mouldings on the ceilings and the doors were not those of a farm house. Bells which had once been rung to summon a servant were in every room and the whole house in its broken-down dejection had kept its miniature grandeur. The living-room was panelled in pine, varnished bright ginger-colour, the fashion in Victorian days. All the rooms were small; a narrow winding staircase led to the first floor and to the cell-like attics where the staff had had to sleep. There were six bedrooms without counting those poor servants' rooms. The house smelled of cats. In the kitchen a row of black iron pots stood on the range. A cat jumped out of one of the giant saucepans and the heads of small kittens looked over the edge. A row of black bells, long since disconnected to the rooms, hung on the wall of the kitchen. The passage to the kitchen was so dark that all that could be seen was a heavy drape of sacking hanging from the ceiling.

On one of the bedroom doors strong kick-marks were indented. After the Duke had abandoned his folly, a man and his wife called Alexandrina and Thomas Barclay had lived there. It is said they were always quarrelling and Thomas Barclay would lock Alexandrina into her room. Alexandrina in her fury had nearly knocked a hole in the door.

That day the house was cold and so dark I could hardly see. The beech trees continued their endless but gentle tapping against the windows; tapping from the breeze from the sea. But in that dank house I felt strangely happy. A happiness I cannot describe. Light over dark. Children had lived there, and in spite of tragedy, happiness prevailed.

Outside, all that could be heard was the cawing of the rooks in the pines. The garden was on a steep slope. At one time it must have been very pretty in its Victorian Scottish way. Now all that was left were overgrown box hedges with spindly legs. Half-dead apple and plum trees still stood, twisted by age and the wind. Columbines were in flower, dotted here and there. The retired grieve of the farm kept an allotment, digging and weeding with his dog by his side. A huge holly hedge, perhaps eighty feet high, divided the steep bank from the house, acting as a wind-break and shelter from the terrible storms which often tear through the land from the sea or from the south-west.

Anthea and I left Skelbo to continue with the packing

up and disembowelling of Innisaonar. I had had a glimpse of Skelbo now and I did not realize what a binding relationship that would turn out to be.

My father's executors were in doubt about allowing me, at twenty-one years old and unmarried, to keep anything at all. But I was determined. I bought Skelbo House and the jungled garden, the ruined castle and the old house, a green wooden boat from one of the hill lochs to use on the sea Loch Fleit, and a rod on the small River Carneigh. I wanted to keep the farm too; a good arable farm of five hundred acres. But it was the main farm on the estate and they said it would have spoilt the sale. My father's executors could not imagine me running a farm and taking a course at an agricultural college, which is what I would have liked to have done. I bought what I managed to extract from them for five hundred pounds. I felt fortunate to have anything.

I spent restless nights in my room in London at the thought of what I had now got. The responsibility and the task of making Skelbo into a home and the fear of doing it alone. Often it would have been easier, a great burden off my mind not to have it at all, but it was a challenge and it had a pull which would not leave me alone.

The next summer I went with Margaret to stay in Dornoch, the nearest town, to arrange for the elementary alterations to be done to the house. There was no electricity. I said I would be content without but the executors insisted that I have it installed. Water came from a ram several fields away. It pumped like a great heart on its own energy, received from a source called the Shepherd's Well; driving the water up to the cattle troughs, to the farm buildings and cottages and to the house.

Margaret did not like to go into the house, her main fear being that bats might be hanging from the old sackcloth in the kitchen passage. She sat firmly on the steep bank outside the house contemplating, almost meditating, on some samples of wallpaper. We went for walks together on the beach at Little Ferry. We sat in the dunes looking out to the sea and to the wreck of the old coal ship which had sunk in that perilous strip of water on the hidden sand-bank. Margaret seemed afraid of the open spaces. She had not been well since our father's death and suffered from a kind of agoraphobia. Also the terns were nesting. They followed us along the beach, screaming at us to go away, swooping low, actually brushing our heads with their wings and pecking at our heads. We were intruders and they were protecting their nests. They hovered over us, keeping our pace, their wings motionless and then suddenly diving to attack us. Twice we went flat on our faces in the sand as though bombs were dropping. One day we saw on the horizon a great white cloud advancing towards us. The sea was ominously quiet. The cloud grew in size as it drew nearer, travelling at enormous speed and changing colour to pink as it reached and obscured the sun. In a few moments we were enveloped by it: this gigantic cloud which seemed like the smoke of cannons tinged with their fire, covering the landscape as well as the sea, the landscape of hills and arable land. It rolled over Skelbo and the shanty-like group of houses on the other side of Little Ferry. The piers disappeared and it went on over Loch Fleit and far into the valleys of the hills, relentless and threatening. There was complete silence. Margaret and I were lost in it and we were afraid.

*   *   *

It was the following year before Skelbo was ready to be lived in. The house was bare of furniture: what had come from Innisaonar was too large for the small rooms and

unsuitable for the architecture of the house. I had beds
and some chairs and a table which was enough to make a
start. I was so afraid of what I had taken on. The thought
ruled me night and day as though the house had taken
hold of me.

Daphne came with me the first time. We had been
brought up together as children in the 'house of light' and
had always remained very close. After arriving at Inverness by train from London we drove the sixty-five miles
to Skelbo. Outside, the house still had its hidden and
secret look which it has never lost but now its window-
frames and doors were painted white. That night we
found that although there was electricity no one had
thought of the practical necessity for electric light bulbs.
In the darkness we hunted amongst the unpacked tea-
chests and trunks until we found some candles. We were
both tired and afraid although the house still had that
atmosphere almost of gaiety in the darkness. Daphne and
I crept about, nearly setting fire to a dresser on which we
had placed some candles. As I went to bed I saw through
the alcove of my turreted bedroom the lighthouse of
Tarbet Ness flashing its light three times at intervals to
show up that peninsular across the sea.

The next day my uncle from the 'house of light' arrived,
bringing in the back of his car young alder and rowan
trees which he had dug from the roadside. He called the
rowans 'anti-spook trees' and said that every house in
Scotland should have one planted near to the building
in order to keep away evil spirits.

The garden, the sea and the loch, the farm and the
surrounding country of water and of hills all have a melancholy, undefinable but present even on a day full of sun.
It is a place full of changes of light, the shape of the
landscape varied as few others. And it is locked-away.

Jamie came to stay. He sat at breakfast, dressed in his

pyjamas and macintosh, reading women's journals. The rest of the day he was inclined to spend in bed. He was a pianist without a piano and he was not content until we found him an upright Bechstein in the Royal Golf Hotel in Brora twelve miles away. Much to Jamie's distaste my uncle made him work. He was persuaded to move great boulders in an effort to make the beginnings of a garden. With his enormous strength it was easy for Jamie but he did it reluctantly. My uncle – that thin, tall, stooping figure with his long-drawn-out, stuttering voice; with his passion for creating gardens; his delight in living uncomfortably; his shrewd and practical mind and with all the pleasures of the senses buried deep within him – he controlled us all. He had a gentle and humorous way of creating order out of chaos. He made life enjoyable and full of meaning. As I write I mourn him.

All food and milk had to be fetched from the towns of Dornoch and Golspie. Mrs. Murray from the farm came to do the cooking. She was a friend, having worked for many years at Innisaonar. She was large and had the strength of a man. She had more the makings of an engineer than that of a cook. The meals she made were almost inedible; haggis and turnips half-cooked.

There were the days of the gale. It was more than a gale. It was a hurricane. It came as suddenly as it left, leaving its destruction behind it. No one could go outside. They would have been knocked over. There was no time for rain. The sea turned into a dark-grey boiling mass. The water appeared in a turmoil. The branches of trees were outstretched like people trying to cling to one another in a disastrous situation. Their arms were rigid and motionless as the hurricane screamed through them. The hurricane did not moan, it shrieked on one long note. There was no movement from anything, just the shrieking and shrieking. The house did not tremble on its solid foundations but we feared almost for our lives. It was at night that we heard the thuds as the trees came down, losing their battle against the hurricane. I was afraid that they would fall on the house and I was afraid of losing the trees. I had previously marked with white paint those which had to be felled, so that light and air could be let into the house. In front of the turrets I had cleared a space so that Loch Fleit and the sea could be seen, also the hills with their individual shapes, which are called Creag Amail, Ben Bhraggie and the Silver Rock, as well as the lighthouse which lay to the south. The house stood high overlooking them all. Had I let in too much of a passage-way for the gales? The next morning I hardly dared to look outside. The country had been ravaged. The shriek-ing had stopped and a calm had descended. It was as though we were surveying the dead after a battle. A huge beech tree lay sprawling down the bank in front of the house, its roots pointing high in the air, making a crater in the ground. The small insects and creatures who lived in the bole of the tree were on the move. Fallen alders and larches lay blocking the drive. We could do nothing to clear the devastation and the foresters all over the county had too much work. My uncle immediately made me a list of trees to be planted that autumn. He regarded the matter as a serious one. 'One day you will wake to find yourself bare of trees,' he said.

It was he who started my passion for planting trees and for watching every morning from my window to see how they had grown during the night. Although it is so hard, I must continue to write about Skelbo and its new awakening and with its trees growing inside me.

*   *   *

I was waiting for Martin to arrive. When the others had gone I rose at dawn and drove to Inverness to meet him. I got there early for the London train and I sat on the station platform smelling the salty air. I was excited. I had known Martin now for three years. We had often talked about marriage but our situation had always remained the same. He had, during that period, gone on long adventures abroad and the months during his absence I had felt a depression and a sense of loss. There was a continual wondering as to what would happen between us. My excitement grew as the train drew in and when I saw him stepping on to the platform wearing his flowing green coat. We had breakfast of smoked haddock and poached eggs in the Station Hotel where the old-fashioned waitresses recognize their regular customers.

The drive from Inverness to Sutherland is not interesting. It takes two hours to Skelbo and longer if one follows the coast. Instead, take Struie Hill, a short cut across the land. It is a huge, bare moor with rolling hills reminiscent of parts of Perthshire. It is what Gunn used to call 'dirty country'. The moment I reach Bonar Bridge and enter the county of Sutherland I feel at home. I take the road fourteen miles across a moor but the landscape has changed. The setting is small, the hills individual, the road narrow with passing places for cars, and grass grows up in patches from under the broken tarmac. Everything is in miniature, even the River Carneigh which flows from Loch Buidhe. The pylons, which are not noticeable in the large landscapes of Scotland, appear too big for this little valley. The land of Innisaonar starts at Loch Buidhe but now Skelbo stands on its own. It holds its independence strongly, away from all else, near to the sea.

I think that Martin was slightly bewildered when he first saw the house. It looked strange and slightly comical, standing on its hill above the farm and with the destruction of the hurricane all around it. I had made the house as perfect as I could. I had arranged a dining-room in the little panelled room which I had had stripped of its varnish. The pine walls were now smooth, silver tinged with red. There was a carpet but no curtains, only shutters to block out the night. I had covered an old table from the store-room at Innisaonar with a piece of red felt. I lit a fire and in the bookshelves I had placed three brown empty bottles with their china labels hanging on chains round their necks. Brandy, Whisky, Rum. It made it look more like a dining-room. Martin was critical as to what I had so far done to the house. I had made the drawing-room into too much what that word implies: pale blue silk walls, a hard Victorian button-backed settee covered in lime-green velvet; my water-colour by Wilson Steer and an eighteenth-century table with little spindly legs, its top covered in faded painted flowers which would have been more at home in one of Jane Austen's houses. Martin and I decided to build Skelbo together. In the future it was to take hold of me, to grip me with an obsession to make it as perfect as possible. 'Thou shalt not make unto thee any graven image' – the commandment I disobeyed and which finally had its revenge on me.

During the next few days I tried to show Martin as much as I could. We walked up the tree side of Creag Amail, the hill which rises steeply behind Innisaonar and from Skelbo resembles a lion lying down. We went by Innisaonar, the house now empty and only lived in for the shooting season. We took the way through the larch trees, the wood behind the house. I did not pass by the little house made of twigs and heather and birch trees which like a ritual I had built every year until my father died. When it was finished at the end of the year it looked like the nest of a wren, covered and lined with moss. I knew what state it would be in now.

Instead we followed the sheep path in the opposite direction, through deep heather and bracken, round stunted birch trees and rowans and rocks. At a point in the path there is a precipice of rock where boulders are scattered. Inset in the rock there is a plaque inscribed with the name 'Florinda', and giving the date 1864. No one knows much about Florinda. She had been a young girl who had lived in the district. She was lame but she used to make her way to this particular place to paint water-colours. One day she died there while she was painting, of what I do not know. I see her as a girl with long fair hair, brave and very delicate. Now this place is known as Florinda's Cave. On that day a dead sheep lay amongst the rocks.

The following morning we went to the ruins of Skelbo Castle which stand a field away from the house. Only parts of the outside walls remain, their stone and mortar barely hanging together but surviving winter after winter, overlooking the sea and Loch Fleit. Trees grow in the middle of the ivy-covered walls where rock pigeons and fulmars nest. The old house in the hollow behind the castle walls has been described as 'a dignified example of the latest development of Scottish baronial architecture, when the castellated features such as corbelled turrets were being dropped'. The gypsies who had long since left their encampment had done much damage during their stay. They had set fire to the roof of the house and had taken many of the timber beams for their fires. I just remember a staircase being there, when the roof and walls were intact. On the first floor innumerable bats used to hang and flutter. Now there is no staircase, only the empty shell of a house; the roof is fast falling in and broken slates lie on the earth floor. On one of the gables there are crude carvings of men with ruffs round their necks. The chimney-stack looks so awry that it would surely topple with the flick of a finger let alone the force of a gale. A visitor, stopping on the track for a moment in the dark before driving up to the house, said that she had begun to shiver at the nearness of the ruins and had to hurry on. It is true there is a heavy gloom and a disagreeable feeling about the castle. This was the place where Scottish chiefs and politicians waited for the Maid of Norway to arrive, watching for her ship to appear on the horizon and sail into Little Ferry. She was to have married the King of Scotland of the time; a good political alliance. She was hardly more than a child and she died before her ship reached its destination.

Martin and I went on down the road which leads to Little Ferry. Here is the narrow mouth where Loch Fleit roars out into the sea. Twice during the day the loch is emptied and filled. When it is empty, stretches of sand lie bare with only a channel of water flowing slowly in and out of the sluice-gates at the head of the loch. The gates have to be opened and shut at regular hours. At the going out of the tide, the waters from the River Fleit and the Carneigh pour through them, and at the coming in the salmon and sea trout run in from the sea and wait for the gates to be opened so that in the summer they can enter the rivers and lay their spawn high up in one of the little pools and burns which flow from the hill. My father was one of the few people who liked it best when the loch was at low tide and oyster-catchers and the small wading birds appeared, waiting and watching and digging their beaks into the sand to see what they could find to eat. There are a few moments at Little Ferry when the water in the outlet is neither coming in nor going out, when the seaweed is motionless, a time of rest. They seem to be minutes of chance before the tide turns once more and the water starts again at dangerous speed. For it is a dangerous place. Ships have come to grief there and it is where the Vikings entered in their longboats, where the Battle of Embo was fought, when the Vikings raped the women, stole the cattle and set fire to the land. They named Little Ferry, Unes, and the country, Sutherland, because to them it was the land of the south.

Many years ago a ferryman rowed people over Little Ferry for a few pence. It was the only way to travel from the town of Golspie to Dornoch until the viaduct road was built by Telford, crossing the far end of the loch. The ferryman died while doing his job. 'The best way to die,' my father used to say. Once Little Ferry was an active place with ships coming in carrying salt and coal. The salt was kept in a storehouse called The Girnal and the coal was unloaded into carts drawn by horses. There is a strong stone pier at Little Ferry and the skeleton of a fishing boat lies beside it. On the Skelbo side the wooden pier is falling to pieces and there are no houses, only the beach and the sand-dunes. That day the tide was going out and Martin and I watched big rafts of black and white eider-duck sitting effortlessly on the water as they were swept out to sea. They looked a little comical to us and also smug as they had their free ride. Seals are often there, either sunning themselves on the sand-banks in the loch or drifting with the tide, their black faces looking inquisitively around, seemingly smiling, and as though they were wearing tight black bathing-caps. Before reaching the sea we crossed a small stony bay and in the distance a patch of empty mussel-shells lay like a bed of gentians. The beach lies round the corner of the bay and it stretches for miles; gold and silver sand and with the gulls calling. We found a straw fisherman's basket lying amongst the sea-weed and the drift-wood, and we filled it with shells and stones: the pink twin shells known as Venus Ears, empty cockles, razor shells and the white worn carapace of the sea-urchin embroidered with a pattern of minute holes;

the stones are striped and under the clear icy water their subdued colours show bright. When the basket was full we carried it back to Skelbo. From Little Ferry, the house and garden appear a perfect half-circle hidden in foliage, giving nothing away.

*　　*　　*

During that winter in London I bought Kit. She was a very small Abyssinian kitten. I saw her in a pet shop and she was the runt of the litter. She had a long pedigree and her official name was Sapphira. I was not intending to buy a cat but when I saw this small creature I took her immediately. Abyssinians are supposed to be the nearest to the ancient Egyptian cat. They have fur like a brown rabbit but each hair is tipped with black. On top of their ears they have small tufts and their stomachs are a pink colour like that of a hare. For a cat-show this little kitten would not have qualified because on her chest she had a few impermissible white hairs. I carried her away in a basket and went to lunch in a café. At once she showed her character. She was independent, playful and a little sly. She cried loudly in the café.

The winter progressed. I began to collect things for Skelbo. Any new acquisition I stored for the time when I would return.

I went back to Skelbo with Martin in June. Yellow gorse was flowering in all the fields. We took Kit with us. She became a huntress. In the morning we would find offerings of field mice heads outside our door; small birds fluttering wounded round the rooms, their blood staining the curtains, and a maimed rabbit dying under the bed.

It was the time of the midnight sun. The bank in front

of the house was covered in high feathery grasses of many different kinds and studded with the flowers of late narcissi and the star of Bethlehem. We walked in Skelbo Glen. It is the place where a Duke of Sutherland had planted every tree he was advised would grow so far north on the east. Once it had been a planned walk beautifully kept but now it has gone wild. The huge conifers only green at the top, trees dead, deformed or struck by lightning. The deciduous trees were just coming out, their leaves as Gunn once said, 'no larger than a mouse's ear'. A burn runs through the glen which used to feed the old water-mill for the farm. Under a wooden bridge we saw an otter at play. We walked in the glen at midnight. It was still bright with the light of the pretended day. Endless days except for a few short hours. It was a time to be happy.

Another evening we drove to the River Fleit. On one side there is the alder wood mixed with old Caledonian pine. This is a marshy place and also suffocating because no wind blows and insects brush your face. On the other side of the river are alders, too, but on the ground a carpet of white garlic flowers spreads like snow. Marsh marigolds and mint and wild iris grow beside the river. It was midnight again. Martin and I lay together amongst the iris and the alder trees. The place looked like a soft bed, a sleeping place for the gods, but the leaves of the iris, the stones underneath them and the twigs of the alder lacerated my body with wounds as sharp as a knife.

The next day we walked to a small loch hidden away in the hills. There is an island in the middle of the loch; marshy with twisted trees and reeds. It looks like a Chinese painting. We lay naked in the sun and watched a pair of greenshanks who were nesting on the island.

This was the place where in a terrible storm of thunder and lightning my father made me take off anything metal on my body and instead of sheltering in the fishing hut with its iron roof we lay under an upturned wooden boat. But that was years ago.

Martin and I had tried to clear the devastation of the last year's hurricane with the help of an old man, Donald Murray, the husband of Mrs. Murray who worked in the house. He had retired from the farm, and together with the help of one of his sons, we did much work. We blew up the roots of the beech tree with gunpowder and on the stumps of the fallen trees we put pots of geraniums to make it look a little like a garden. Martin started to dig a terrace in front of the house. We took fallen stones from the walled fields and the castle ruins. He and Donald Murray built a wall, and underneath, a border fifteen feet wide which I was to plant in the coming autumn. A grass path was to lead along the border and we spent days with Donald Murray digging sea-washed turf from the small bay at Little Ferry. We cut it into squares like the best turf cutters do with a special tool, and Donald Murray would lift it from the ground and I would load it into the back of the car. It was the best sea-washed turf as used for croquet lawns, and we were told that it would take fifty years to grow again. It was a long, hard job and we worked long hours. Sea-pinks grew in the turf and each square had to be laid and joined like a jigsaw puzzle. 'A puckle of sand,' said Donald Murray sprinkling each join in the turf.

After we had laid the grass, Martin went away for a while. I spent three weeks alone at Skelbo. I was not independent. I was dependent on the house. I was building a home, perhaps too early in my life, but I had already done much wandering. I lived unafraid there and never locked a door at night. I was happy in the house and everything I saw and touched took on a meaning for me. I stood outside, smelling the smoke from the log fire which curled its way out of the tall chimney between the two little turrets.

TO THE PLACE OF SHELLS

The house has a smell of its own; of pine wood and clean air and the smoke of the birch logs.

One night I was woken by a loud clattering noise. It sounded as though saucepans were being thrown all round the kitchen; banging and crashing. I got out of bed. I took hold of the steel poker from the fireplace and gripped it very hard. I crept down the stairs. Would I be able to deal with the situation? I made my way to the kitchen and opened the door very slowly. Something hurled itself against the closed window. It shot past me, nearly knocking me over. It was a huge cat, almost demented with fear. I just had a glimpse of this wild animal tearing down the passage and leaping through an open window. It was no ordinary cat. I have heard that wild cats very occasionally come down from the rocks and the hill to the arable land. I imagined that Kit had attracted this cat from the hill and that she had been raped. She looked contented and undisturbed. For many days a strong pungent smell hung round the house. This must have been a wild cat and not just a farm cat gone wild, for there was none. The desperate fear it showed at being trapped in a house and seeing a human being moved me greatly. The fear in wild animals makes me weep. I feel so close to them.

Martin returned for a few days. The endless question of marriage was discussed without conclusion. Should I break my tie with him? We quarrelled. We drove to Ben Hope. That enormous hump of a hill which lies near the most northern coast appeared unfriendly in spite of the fairy-like road bordering Loch Hope. The rowan trees were scarlet with berries; the birches turning yellow; the mosses soaking with the autumn.

Martin still worked with Donald Murray. Mrs. Murray still cooked inedible meals cheerfully and like a strong man in the kitchen. Wild geese whined over the house every evening, honking and honking. Their call of departure gave me shivers down my spine. 'When the geese go south I go too,' said Martin to Donald Murray. The old man looked puzzled.

I drove Martin to Inverness to catch the train. I was to stay and plant the border and work. This time I did not want to be left alone. I clung to him and we quarrelled again. Rain poured down on the hill road from Loch Buidhe on my return. It was dark, with neither moon nor stars. The headlights of the car illuminated the eyes of the sheep and the cattle by the roadside. I saw them as monsters persecuting me. For the first time I was afraid in the middle of that moorland. I looked behind me. There was nobody there. Only the glowing eyes of the sheep and cattle haunting me in the dark and the rain. When I reached home the house was in darkness and I felt for that moment it was not my friend.

The following days I planted roses in the new border. They did not begin to fill it. The shrub roses, Blanc Double de Coubert and nine bushes of Nevada near to the pines where the rooks live. The rooks act strangely. They are there for days at a time, busy and reptilian and making a great noise. Then suddenly they disappear, to where I do not know. But they always return. They are part of Skelbo. I was not happy in those days. It was the back-end of the year, my favourite time, but I felt alone. There was only one key to the door and every evening Mrs. Murray's son would lock me into the house so that she could let herself in the next morning. I would watch his tall gangling figure in the semi-darkness through the window. He would always be swinging his axe, of which I was afraid, his maroon-coloured beret askew, as he locked me in for the night and he shambled away amongst the fallen leaves.

*   *   *

The birth of Kit's kittens was not so ordinary as it sounds. No other cats can replace them and now they are gone. Martin kept Kit in his basement flat in Eaton Square. Her kittens were born in a dark cupboard in a box in his bedroom. He delivered them. She had four in all. She was an extremely good mother. How strange is the gait of a cat as it carries its young by the scruff of the neck, the weight of the kittens making them swing like a pendulum; their little bear-like faces with rounded ears and their eyes tightly closed. As they grew older we could see how different they were. One was a true Abyssinian and very pretty and feminine. We gave her to friends who called her Abyssinia. It was possible to tell immediately that the other two were not ordinary. One grew huge and he had about him a sulky wildness that was utterly misplaced in a city. It was plain that he came from the hill. He was a dull brown colour, coarse and clumsy. He also incorrigibly wet his bed. We gave him to an American girl who called him Haile and took him to New York. We kept the runt of the litter who was small and dependent and was more grey in colour than Kit. He did not hiss so much as the others and was utterly defenceless.

We were going to Skelbo for Easter. A few days before, this little kitten got lost. We spent our time searching and pasting notices for a lost kitten on the railings of houses and embassies. We put Kit in her basket and were sadly leaving for the train in the evening when there was a screaming and crying and the kitten came running into the room, his tail pointed high and wagging it like a dog. He must have got locked in at the top of the tall house, and had it been five minutes later we would have lost him for ever. We put him into the cat basket and with our luggage, which always looked like a tinker's load, we got into a taxi. 'Liverpool Street,' said Martin to the driver. He too had been confused and miserable by the loss of the kitten. After some time we realized it was Euston we should go to and we caught the train with two minutes to spare.

At Skelbo the bank under the trees was covered in small wild daffodils. When they are very old some of the flowers open green. They look unnatural and give one an uneasy feeling. They call them Lent lilies.

Charlotte and Evelyn came to stay with their small daughter. We took them to gather mussels when the tide was out. Large mussel beds lie within reach and we waded into the loch to collect them. They cling together in groups in various sizes, some no bigger than a baby's fingernail, others fat and full. Martin made soup of them.

I was envious of Charlotte and Evelyn's close and happy marriage. Evelyn was kind to me and helped me plant lavender in the hard earth by the house. 'And some fell upon stony ground,' I said to him, laughing.

*   *   *

Martin and I spent the early summer travelling in North Africa in search of remote Roman ruins. A few weeks after our return we married in the small chapel of St. Peter's, Eaton Square. We went to Norderney in the German Friesland Islands for our honeymoon. The sky and the wind and the deserted beaches with their sand dunes were the same as at Little Ferry.

Afterwards we went straight to Skelbo. It was August, my least favourite month, when the grass is rank and the weeds are seeding; ragwort appears and the best of the roses are over; when the hills are covered in purple heather which to me seems to give the country a touch of vulgarity.

Archie came to stay. As soon as he arrived I fell ill

with a high fever. Dr. MacKenzie from Dornoch was called. He is a doctor of the old school, gruff and forthright. I became worse, with bouts of shivering cold. Archie came to sit by my bed. He was a quiet and gentle companion. He gave to Martin and me as a wedding present a copy of Manzoni's *I Promessi Sposi*, which he had translated into English. I see him sitting by my bed, the room all white with the alcoves of the turrets covered in an old wallpaper of flowers and birds which semed so alive that I felt I could pick them off the walls; the white muslin curtains with their small diamond pattern, floating and billowing in the slight breeze from the sea; the large Dresden figures of 'Night' and 'Day' on their stands on the wall; the tall picture of the Virgin and Child above my bed. I liked Archie sitting beside me. He was a convert to Roman Catholicism and lived in a secluded community in Kent. We had peaceful conversations.

Eventually I became so ill that I was taken by ambulance to an isolation hospital in Inverness. No one knew what was wrong with me. In Tunisia, while Martin was looking at a Roman ruin and the heat had been too great for me to explore it with him, a Bedouin woman appeared with a dirty tin of goat's milk to refresh me. It was warm and thick and full of lumps. I thought it would be rude for me to refuse it although it was so nauseating that it was almost impossible to swallow. The milk and tin must have been full of germs because eventually the hospital discovered that I had a rare African infection.

Martin and Archie drove every day the long way to Inverness to see me. Martin took him to the Strathpeffer Games. I could not imagine Archie amongst the candyfloss and the wrestlers and the weight-throwers. I felt sorry for Archie on his holiday. I felt a failure as a hostess to him. I spent three weeks in the hospital and he had to leave before I could return.

I was happy in those days. There seemed to be more point, now that Martin and I were married, in building a home and we shared an enthusiasm to make Skelbo as perfect as possible. Mrs. MacAlastair from the farm came to help Mrs. Murray. She took over the cooking and produced delicious meals. For breakfast there was a bowl of dark brown eggs from her hens and the coffee was good and strong. On sunny days Martin would play classical music on the gramophone. The house was filled with the joyful music he chose. Kit went on with her hunting much to my distaste, and her kitten grew to an enormous size. He had a thick bushy tail like a fox and his ears were blunt and rounded like a wild cat's. He had the vulnerability of a slightly backward child and continued to feed from his mother until he was almost fully grown. We simply called him 'Tom'. Sometimes the cats would fight in anger or in play. Screams could be heard as they bit one another and fur would fly and lie in little tufts on the floor. Tom was extremely cautious about entering a room. If he sensed that strangers were present he would open the ajar door with his paw and peer through it with his big sad eyes. If there was anyone foreign to him he would run with his tail fluffed out to another part of the house. He did not enjoy hunting. He did so because he was taught by his mother and he seemed to think it his duty as a cat. He would catch a mouse without harming it and watch it dart from one corner to another. Once he carried a large pullet all the way up the hill from the farm and let it run by my bed. It belonged to the shepherd's wife and she was not pleased. Tom would lie on the bed or behind a warm radiator, flat on his back with his hind legs open in abandonment and with a look of ecstasy on his face. He had no independence. He remained like a lost child, timid and affectionate. How I loved my cats with their different characters: Kit with her sly independent ways and her little smiling face which had been caused by Martin playing bean-bag with her when she was a kitten. She had caught the bean-bag in her mouth and it pulled her tooth sideways and it never went back again. And Tom with his innocent eyes, puzzled and fearful. Tom always came for walks with me. I tried to leave him behind but he would not be left alone. We walked up the hard earth track from the house and after a short way he would cry to be picked up and carried because the ground was hurting his paws. He was heavy and he insisted on being carried like a baby, his head resting in the crook of my arm. One day he rashly went into a pen of ewes. The ewes crowded in on him angrily. They stamped their feet, making a hollow sound on the ground. They could have become nasty and I feared for my unaware Tom. He was truly no ordinary cat. The sun shone in those days. Now there is loss in my heart.

*   *   *

It was the first Christmas we spent at Skelbo. I tell it in a simple way because that is how it was. There was no snow there but in the far distance Ben Klibreck could be seen shining white in the sun. It was the hill that William and I always called the breast hill so like a perfect breast in shape it was. At Skelbo it was grey and perfectly still and the little sea birds such as the sanderlings flocked in their white winter plumage. I decorated the house with holly cut from the old hedge which that year was covered in scarlet berries. Owls hooted at the end of the short day of Christmas Eve. The land and the sea were calm as it began to grow dark; it was as though they were waiting for the miracle of the following day.

Above the white curtain pole with its pale yellow velvet

curtains I made a thick border of holly. Martin had a special liking for nineteenth-century Gothic and we had papered the walls in the dining-room in a blue and brown version, a copy from Horace Walpole. There was holly on the sideboard, an ornate piece of furniture, gold, pink and blue with a marble top; holly mixed amongst tangerines and sugared fruits; mistletoe hung in the hall. We kissed. A tall Christmas tree was placed in the drawing-room. Margaret and I covered it in silver balls and tinsel and candles. We laid the table in the dining-room with a white cloth and on it we placed the iced Christmas cake, meringues and all kinds of sweet things for the children at the farm. In every space there was a cracker and bunches of balloons hung from the curtain pole. There were presents for everyone and a present each day for Martin for the twelve days of Christmas. Wallace MacLeod, the retired postman who also operated the sluice-gates at the head of Loch Fleit, came to act as Father Christmas in an ill-fitting costume. The little children filed in, their cheeks scarlet with the cold and excitement. They sat silently at the table eating until every cake was finished. One small boy had a false nose in his cracker which made the others begin to talk and laugh. Martin organized the games and there was a treasure hunt all over the house. I was strong and happy but there was a gap to be filled. The gap of our own child.

That New Year's Eve was one never to be repeated. It is the custom there for people to go from house to house to drink and eat a special kind of currant bun. They call it 'first footing'. We were about to go to bed when there was a loud knocking at the door. Outside was the retired grieve from the farm with his wife and son. We were clearly not the first house they had visited. They all sat in the drawing-room drinking whisky. Jonathan MacLean, the old man, squeezed my arm and my knee. I wished that they had not come. It seemed customary to stay as long as possible, to the dawn even, and to become more and more incoherent. Martin produced a bottle of green chartreuse and unwisely gave it to Jock MacLean, who was only sixteen. Martin explained to him that it was made by Carthusian monks. 'Monkeys,' said Jock laughing, tipping back the bottle. Suddenly he turned white in the face and vomited all over the velvet settee. Mrs. MacLean, as if to protect her son, immediately sat on it covering it with her voluminous skirts. Jock recovered, but the settee never did in spite of its being washed and scrubbed. Mrs. Murray and Mrs. MacAlastair walked through the dark up to the house and hustled them furiously away. As he went out Jock was sick again all over the curtains in the passage. 'Monkeys,' he said in a faint voice as he left. I worked most of the night trying to clear up the mess in my delicate boudoir. No one present ever referred to the matter again.

Martin and I had decided to make the little panelled room with its pine walls into our main sitting-room. We put in a marble fireplace where we could have an open fire. We collected things all the winter in London. Martin complained that anything good we acquired went to Skelbo. The room as well as the house started to consume me. The small panelled room with its little double doors became one of natural colours; silver and green and cream. The room is all windows with two little windows in the rounded alcoves of the turrets. Cream velvet curtains flow endlessly in front of the shutters. Chairs and the sofa and a round table seem to melt effortlessly into place. On the shelves in the wall Martin placed a great stuffed snowy owl and shells and stones and the white bones of birds from the beach. He stuck butterflies on pins into the wood. Row after row of little foreign butterflies and moths decorated the shelves. Above the marble fireplace we hung a picture called *The Lute Player* by Etty. It shows three ladies with a lute player; a feather in his hat as he plays on the balcony. The picture is in Venetian colours and is in a glowing tortoise-shell frame. Above is an old carved head of a thin stag. Its antlers are real; it has a garland of flowers round its neck and its ears flop sadly like a hind in distress. Once it had been brightly painted but now with all the paint worn away it is bone-coloured like the tone of that alive but peaceful room.

*   *   *

Martin was not content with the wall and terrace which he and Donald Murray had built. It looked too amateur. I was determined to make as beautiful a garden as possible in spite of the hard climate and the salty winds. We employed dry-stone wallers to lay the grey stones supporting the terrace. The wall leads for several hundred yards from the cornfields beside the house, along to the pines where the rooks live, towards the little storage house which was once the laundry. They also built pink sandstone steps to divide the border and Martin ordered pine logs and set them into the grass to lead the way down the steep hill behind the old holly hedge. The sheltered lower part of the garden we were to leave until later. At the moment it remained a jungle. For weeks and months I studied gardening catalogues and books, dreaming of a garden, gazing fixedly at each tree and rose and flower I might see. A garden beyond reality. I filled the border with pink and silver shrubs and roses, grouping each in threes and fives, colour against colour as a choreographer might arrange a ballet. I planted *regale* lilies, too, amongst a brownish rose.

TO THE PLACE OF SHELLS

I had always had a dream of a garden beyond reality. There would have been no grass or anything green. High walls would surround it, making a perfect square. To hide the walls, dark copper beeches would be planted and the paths would be of red gravel. Any flower or shrub in this garden would be of a purple species, dark in colour like red sedum or black fennel. Not one green leaf or blade of grass would grow there. The darkness it would produce would be that of twilight or like a garden dripping in blood.

Instead, my garden was all green with grass and trees of no particular shape, not rigid but flowing in its natural contours. That is what I was given to make and form with my hands.

Margaret and I lay in the lower part of the garden amongst the high grass before the bulldozers came to destroy the enchantment of that place. She told me how, during her stay at Skelbo, she was woken at five o'clock every morning by the sound of hobnailed boots on the flagstone kitchen floor directly below her room. She wondered why Donald Murray was active so early and then she heard the slamming of the door of the old iron kitchen-range which was now bricked up. One morning she felt a presence in her room. It was of a rough farming man. All she could see were his reddish brown stockings but without any doubt his presence was there and he stayed for several minutes. She had not been at all afraid because his company had been friendly. Without hearing Margaret's story Mrs. Murray had said that one night when she was sleeping in the house while I was alone, she, too, had been woken at five o'clock in the morning. She had heard the same hobnailed boots on the kitchen floor and the same slamming of the kitchen-range door below the same bedroom. It must have been the old coachman coming in early to light the range for his employers. The presence in the room must have been that of the tenant farmer who committed suicide. I do not hear or see such things but Skelbo is haunted with a light happiness. It is a house full of tragedies transcended by what I do not know. I experienced a moment of intense joy as I lay with Margaret in the long grass. I was full of emotion as I saw such beauty, looking up at the blue sky and watching an occasional butterfly pass in flight over our faces. The garden, the cornfields, the loch and the sea all seemed in harmony. I love Skelbo so much that I am almost moved to tears as I think of that afternoon.

We ploughed up the land and moulded it into the shape we wished. Now in the lower part of the garden there is a short walk under the holly hedge which is planted with an avenue of round-headed whitebeams. Underneath the trees I planted the rose, Prosperity, and two long beds of the deep purple rose, Reine des Violettes. I made many mistakes and dug up what I had planted and re-planted with more hardy shrubs. Over the old plum tree I tried the rose, New Dawn, which hangs with its silver-pink flowers blooming all the summer. More log steps lead from a gap in the holly hedge down to the little potting-shed with its pointed slate roof. What was then the long grass where Margaret and I lay is now a steep slope of lawn. Everywhere we dug, whisky bottles were turned up from the earth, a relic from the tenant farmer. Donald Murray brought in all kinds of objects. One day it was a beautiful brass plate inscribed with the words: 'Duke of Sutherland. Number 6.' It was one of the plates attached to the farm carts when horses were used. Another day a small brass stamp for writing-paper was found. 'Skelbo House, Dornoch, Sutherlandshire', it said. It must have been a ducal relic as it is many years since the county has been called Sutherlandshire. But I cannot imagine the Duke and his guests writing long letters in his folly. As we planted grass seed and turned the space at the side of the house back into a lawn and dug up tree stumps, Donald Murray told us many times how he was just able to remember Daisy, Countess of Warwick, playing croquet there.

Not long ago there had been a small train which joined the main line to the north. It went from Meall station where the sluice-gates are and round Loch Fleit, passing through level-crossing gates at Innisaonar, Camus and Skelbo. Skelbo had a station of its own: a small platform and a hut on which hung an old pair of stag's antlers covered in lichen. Then the train went on through Embo to Dornoch. The train had a steam-engine and because of its long funnel we called it 'the coffee-pot'. There being no buses, the train was used by many people and carried all the farming materials. The first-class carriages had red plush seats and it was often possible to get a free ride. When we were children we placed pennies on the line, the same penny over and over again until it was no more than a paper-thin piece of metal. Some years ago the train was abolished, the lines taken up, the level-crossing gates were removed and the gate cottages where the gate-keepers lived put up for sale. We bought the Skelbo gate cottage. It was a little brick square cottage built about the time when the railway was brought to the north. Several hundred yards of railway line went with it which we exchanged with the farm for a plot of land to be used as a vegetable garden. Donald Murray was getting frail and although he still worked for a few hours a day in the garden we needed someone there when we were away. We rough-cast the cottage white and did many alterations and added a small greenhouse. We found a gardener and his wife called Fraser. Mrs. Murray now went to work in the school in Dornoch but she remained a constant visitor to the house. Her life was hard, looking after Donald Murray and her brother and her two rough sons. She also milked the cow on the farm. She had to dress as a man when she milked because this particular cow did not like women. Every time she milked her Mrs. Murray had to wear a man's cap and coat and trousers to prevent the cow from kicking over the pail.

The Fraser family moved into the cottage. James Fraser was a small man with red hair who ran everywhere. We could not stop him from running as he worked or while we asked him to do something.

I did not feel my time wasted building up Skelbo. My days were not empty or sterile. All I lacked was a child. I craved for a child to fill the spaces at Skelbo. I bought a swing to hang on a tree by the old laundry for other children to play with. On a walk beside Loch Buidhe with Martin, I broke down. I could see no way further without a child. Skelbo needed children as much as myself. It was once a child's paradise. Almost every picture we bought in London was of a mother and child. It seemed to compensate a little to be crowded by these images. Most of the guests who came to stay brought their children with them. How I longed for one to be mine.

Martin's favourite period was the 1830s, a little earlier than the house. In a sale-room in London he found for twenty pounds a portrait of a mother with her child. It is a large portrait and was painted by an Irish artist, Richard Rothwell. The child is sitting naked on her mother's knee and the colours are of dark bitumen, golden yellow and mauves like black currants and cream. We also bought a round painting by Etty called *The Three Sisters*. It shows the girls in a group, their long slender necks bending towards each other. Most of the other pictures were water-colours of children painted in good amateur style. We collected hand-coloured prints by William Daniell which show early scenes of Sutherland and Caithness and the surroundings where we lived.

*　　*　　*

One summer Christian came to stay. Christian felt at
home in Sutherland. He was a young man but looked
even younger than he was. He spent his life painting in
water-colours and oils. He took his art seriously and lived
for it. Before he came to us he rented a cottage owned by
an actor who lived some miles away. The actor was a
huge figure with a beard, who practised falconry. Any
day on a visit to Dornoch one could see him in the shops
with his Land-Rover parked outside. In the back of the
Land-Rover were his hooded falcons looking medieval,
and occasionally I heard the falconry bells tinkling clear
in the distance. But Christian was lonely and gave up the
cottage and came to stay at Skelbo. He painted mostly
landscapes and tried to sell his pictures to whoever might
call at the house. He was a person full of strange but
inventive ideas. He decided that in the future people were
going to travel by a kind of electric parachute. He made a
model out of linen and wire which took him hours to
construct. Late at night he would take it up to the attic
above our bedroom to fly it and he made a great noise.
He also practised yoga and whenever I entered the little
panelled room I might find him standing on his head. I
liked Christian but there was about him some slight
touch of animal cunning. Something not quite human.
He had wanted to spend the winter living in the castle
ruins. Martin did not see any reason why he should not;
I knew that he would die from exposure.
　　Sometime after, Christian hanged himself in London.

*　　*　　*

Another Christmas came. . . . It was a Christmas such as I have never seen at Skelbo. The snow was deep and hard and there was sun during each short day. I carried out the Christmas rituals with great care and happiness. I cut holly while I listened to carols on the wireless. I produced traditional meals and there were presents and stockings for everyone. Rachel and Ian came to stay with their baby and nurse. We took them up to Loch Buidhe which was frozen with several inches of ice. We slid far across the loch surrounded by the snow-covered hills, not knowing how dangerous it could be because the burns with their undercurrents do not stop running into the loch. All troubles were abandoned for that day. We laughed as we slid and fell. We had brought sleighs in the back of the car and we tobogganed down the hill as fast as we could towards the Thorbol Falls. The birch trees were covered in ice and jingled when they were touched. Trees made of pink shining glass, their old twisted branches motionless in the perfectly still clear air. The Thorbol Falls were static, huge icicles hanging from the precipitous rocks.

Those days were not without difficulties. The pipes from the Shepherd's Well which supplied the house with water had become corroded with age. Suddenly we were without water. The plumber worked long hours but said that nothing could be done. For the first time in my life I realized that it is impossible to exist without water. The local fire-brigade came to fill up the tank, dragging their hoses through the house, but what they supplied only lasted a few hours. I organized a routine which was a full day's work for two people. Large containers were taken down to the farm and filled slowly with one tap which took an hour or so. They were then loaded into the back of the Land-Rover and were driven up the hill, the water slopping over the sides, losing half each time. The water was then fed into a tank in the garden and went up through the electric pump in the kitchen. When the pump worked it was possible to hear the water rising through the pipes in the house to the taps upstairs. What joy it gave me to hear that gurgling noise and to see some water. Playing with water has always held a fascination for me: the ram pumping on its own energy, and when I was a child, building dams in the burn at Innisaonar and breaking them down again. Clearing the burn of sticks and twigs to make it run more freely. Water going up and down, water being diverted in its natural course. Playing with water in different ways. My father held the same passion. Energy from vital water.

Rachel and Ian were uncomplaining guests but it cannot be denied that the lack of water spoiled their visit. When at last the pipes from the Shepherd's Well were persuaded to work again, the Land-Rover froze and the snow became so deep that it could not be driven up the hill. I thawed out the Land-Rover with a hot water-bottle but all food and supplies had to be pulled through the garden gate and up the garden on sleighs.

I gave the same children's party as previously but this time it was not so happy as before. I relied on Martin to help with the games but he had been shooting with friends and retired to bed with a headache. Rachel and Ian and their baby and nurse retreated to their rooms. I felt there to be conflict at Skelbo and that the house was revealing that dark shadow which rarely showed itself.

When Martin went away I asked Gerard to stay. He spent much of his time in bed and ate at irregular hours. He brewed many pots of tea, taking them to his room and covering them with his underpants to act as a tea-cosy. He was both an easy and a difficult guest. I took him for a drive on one of those winter days. I took him along the little road which leads from Golspie and up behind Ben Bhraggie and along down to Rogart. Suddenly a blizzard

TO THE PLACE OF SHELLS

started. It was impossible to see one yard ahead. This is a place where many crofters live but it is a desolate ground. There are no trees and the land is bare with stretches of poor grass and reeds. The snow drove towards us like a great collapsing wall. I did not dare to stop and went on very slowly. We skidded several times. We could have easily have gone off the road and got lost, for there are miles without any crofts. I was anxious but Gerard seemed petrified. He clung to the seat of the car trying not to show panic – Gerard, who had fought in the Spanish Civil War, and who had been captured as a journalist in Norway during the Second World War and was sent to a prison camp where he met Martin and from which he escaped.

*　　*　　*

The steading is where the cattle and sheep shelter for the winter and above their pens a wooden staircase leads to the granary. To put your hands in the huge mounds of corn and to feel the smooth grains trickle through your fingers is to feel a wholeness of oneself. Birds fly in and out and the smell is of the dust of grain and of farm manure and of old wood. The tall doors of the steading are slatted and rounded at the top. Everything was swept clean like a new house for the shooting picnics we had there with my father.

There was to be a sale of produce organized by the factor and his wife. It was to be held in the steading on one summer day. To my horror, without consulting me, they decided that I should open the sale. I only heard about it when I saw my name on a poster in Dornoch. I spent days writing a short speech, worrying unduly about such a small task. I went for walks in the fields rehearsing what I was going to say; speaking out loud to myself the

142

words. It became an increasing nightmare. When the day came Martin and I walked down to the farm. Trestle-tables had been put up with cloths spread over them and on these were bowls of Mrs. MacAlastair's dark brown eggs, cakes and scones and fruit from neighbouring farmers. There was only a handful of people. Everyone from the farm and Wallace MacLeod the retired postman and a few guests. It would have been easier if there had been a crowd unknown to me and I distant on a platform. Now every word went out of my head and to my shame I had to read my speech from my notes. It sounded pompous and formal and unsuited to the occasion. The gathering politely clapped and then thankfully went on with the sale and drank their tea.

There was to be a dance in the steading that evening. It could not have been the first, as Donald Murray said that long ago he could remember 'many a dancer coupling there'. Local farmers and their wives were invited and there was a Scottish band. The dance was held in the granary which was empty at that moment because the corn had not been reaped. The band played Scottish reels, eightsomes and the Gay Gordons, and the dancers whirled their way through them clumsily, hiding their half bottles of whisky in their pockets. All the men wore kilts and the sound of their feet thumped on the granary floor, lit by flickering candles. Faster and faster the music went, well into the night until all were exhausted.

*   *   *

We had invited Marigold and Patrick to stay. They both looked beautiful. Patrick was 'mad, bad and danger-ous to know'. I had never felt at ease with Patrick. Mari-gold, with her green eyes and red hair, was wild and

143

unpredictable. We spent pleasant and innocuous days with them without any trouble. Martin and Patrick fished for cuddies on the old broken pier at Little Ferry. I see them now, with their coats billowing behind them, looking like two comedians. Dangling their hooks and lines in the clear water; fooling and joking as they caught one cuddie after another. Cuddies are a fish resembling a grey mullet and taste like a soft brown trout. I cleaned them and fried them in oatmeal which I found in the larder. The cuddies went blue in the frying-pan. We discovered that the jar which I had thought was full of oatmeal had been left unlabelled by Mrs. Murray and in fact contained rat poison.

There were the days when Marigold would stay in the house and Martin and Patrick went off on expeditions. I used to walk up the River Carneigh and if there was enough water, fish for a grilse or lie in the bracken. The bracken in high summer has a wonderful smell near to bitterness as it grows out of the moss or the heather. Sometimes I lay under a stunted birch looking up through its branches thinking how much it resembled an olive tree. I was always a lazy fisher.

Patrick died a few years back. He was found in his garden with a hypodermic syringe in his arm. He had taken to heroin.

*   *   *

It was the following summer that Martin bought the old dove-cote. It stood twelve feet high on a white-painted fluted column. There were many little holes for the doves to go in and the pointed roof was made of lead. We had it put up by a crane beside the garden gate which leads to the farm. How pretty it looked beside the cherry trees.

Martin bought brown turtle-doves to live in it but they were not strong enough to stand the hard climate. He then tried white pigeons and wired them into the cote until they were used to the place where they should roost. One morning we found a poor headless bird. It must have stuck its head through the wire netting and a hawk had snapped it off. When the rest of the pigeons were acclimatized to their new home we let them out and they flew over the farm and the castle ruins at speed to join the rock pigeons, their wings shining white against the sky. Now they too have disappeared, all but one, and the dove-cote was blown down in a gale, and smashed irreparably.

Suddenly we received a telephone call from Inverness. Two friends had arrived without warning. Peter was a huge man with a great head like that of a Moses, his hair red and curly like thistle-down and everything about him in disorder. He would not go to bed at night and sometimes when one came down to breakfast he would still be dozing in his chair, tobacco from his pipe all around him. When eventually he went to bed he would not get up again until after much persuasion.

We took them along the Princess's Walk, over the black bridge and along the path which leads to the Thorbol Falls. Bracken and moss grow there amongst the trees and young alder bushes. Lichen grows on the old birches and the colours are grey and green. Peter shuffled along, enjoying himself. To me it is the most beautiful walk on earth as you climb over the fallen trees and suddenly find yourself nearly behind the waterfall. When there has been a lot of rain you feel the spray on your face as the water thunders into the brown pool below. Sun catches the water and makes a rainbow. The waterfall is too high for the salmon to leap so a salmon-ladder was built. Small pools lead to join the upper part of the river; the place where the fishers go. Ferns hang low over the pools and patches of white foam gather. Few would guess that the salmon-ladder was man-made, so hidden and over-grown it is. The fish rest in the pools before they leap up one step after another.

It is possible to turn the ladder off so that it runs dry, and my father used to hide the key of the small sluice-gate which controls the water, under the moss in a special place. He turned it off on my birthdays and I would stand in a pool and catch a salmon with my hands. We did it quietly and secretly. We knew it was an unsporting thing to do.

There was to be a sale at Cromarty House. The owner was selling the house and the contents were to be auctioned. Cromarty is a small dying town which stands on the shore of the Cromarty Firth on the tip of what is called The Black Isle. Cromarty leads to nowhere although I believe at one time it had a lace-making industry. It is a long drive from Skelbo but the house is large and Georgian and there was the possibility of buying something good. We went with Veronica and Peter. Peter in his old felt hat and with half a bottle of whisky tucked under his coat. Cromarty House looks over the firth. It was nearly derelict inside. Traces of its past could be seen, with its grand wallpaper peeling and the mouldings on the ceilings and walls cracked and broken. A large crowd had gathered to see what they could find. The room where the auction was held was packed with junk so worthless and ugly that I could not imagine anyone would want it. Every object appeared to have something wrong with it: old buckets with holes in them, broken fire-guards and wicker clothes-baskets. There was not one object of interest. In spite of this, things went for high prices, the auctioneer obviously enjoying himself. I thought it a pity to have come so far without bidding for anything so I bought a navy-blue umbrella which might have come in useful. At the end of the sale Peter could not be found. We searched in the empty rooms which were all of bad Georgian style. It seemed that he had vanished. He had grown tired and had wandered off. We went upstairs to endless other rooms and discovered him at last, asleep in an old armchair in totally bare surroundings. He was comfortably passing the time with his hat tilted over his nose and his half-bottle of whisky beside him. There were two elegant iron seats outside the front door. After much persuasion Martin bought them from the owner. They now stand side by side in the short walk under the holly hedge where the round-headed whitebeams grow.

As we left Cromarty House I put up my umbrella to try it out. Moths fell from it and the whole thing split into holes. I hid it discreetly and furtively behind a bush in the garden.

Veronica and Peter returned to London. Peter left an empty half-bottle of whisky in his bedroom. Mrs. Mac-Alastair was shocked.

*   *   *

I welcomed guests but always felt a sense of relief when they left. It was Martin who wanted a continual flow of people. He never found it tiring because he often left it to me to entertain them. It was definitely a strain because I strove to make it as perfect as possible for them. There were the days when the guests had gone; peaceful restful days when I could tend the garden with which I was becoming more and more obsessed. I still watched every morning from the window to see how some plant or tree had grown overnight: the trees which I had planted: sycamore, beech and elm, chestnut, Spanish chestnut and holly. When a rose failed I tried a new kind in its place. I was beginning to know what would or would not grow at Skelbo. We planted a wood of birches and rowans by the path which leads to the old laundry; I loved to see them budding in the spring. I was creating a garden of grey and green and deep purple. Everytime a plant grew it seemed a miracle. I loved the lazy days when Martin and I were alone with the cats and I would spend my time cutting the dying heads off the roses, dreaming all the time of other miracles. My garden did not blaze, it shone softly before me. As I cut the heads off the fading roses and dropped them into a large flat basket, Tom, who was always by my side, would come and lie in it on a bed of petals of the strong-scented Madame Isaac Pereire or the pale Penelope. He stretched himself out amongst the warm petals and I carried him from bush to bush. He always lay on his back, his hind legs wide apart and with what seemed to be a smile on his face. How I loved those days when I was at one with myself and the garden. The days without trouble. The days of happiness. Can they ever be regained?

I had hoped that Skelbo might be a place where Martin could write, but he was always occupied outside or away in London. If only the farm had been ours. We searched for something which would make Skelbo self-supporting and would interest Martin too but it was always in vain. Martin never rested for long and I did not expect him to. It had not become his country. There were warning signs to which I paid no heed; instead I clung to him when he left, although after partings I became independent again. There were the times when the mist came in from the sea. Occasionally it would last three or four days. The sun would break through for an hour or two and one might catch a glimpse of a hill or the trees before it descended again.

The cats, especially when I was alone, played a large part in life at Skelbo. Tom remained an eternal kitten, looking with his accusing eyes through the panelled room windows, asking to be let in at the slightest drop of rain. There was terrible anxiety if one of them was missing. I would search through the garden and fields and the plantations of wind-breaks. Once I found Tom with his paw in a rabbit snare and he lay for days nursing himself, demanding constant attention. I went to see the rabbit trapper and he promised never to set a trap near Skelbo again. Another time Kit was lost for two days. I called her all over the farm until my voice became hoarse. There must surely be disaster. At last I found her by a small pond near to the mill, sitting in the sun, trying to catch water-boatmen with her paw on the still surface. Departures from Skelbo were always a scene near to catastrophe. 'Lock the cats up,' we would say, but Tom, seeing the wicker travelling basket, would run as fast as he could to a hiding place. Time would grow shorter and shorter if we were to catch the train and still he could not be found. Dressed for London I would search in the fields until I found him sitting watching a pigeon without any intention of catching it. While we drove to Inverness the cats set up a chorus of howling. When one stopped the other would begin. It continued the whole way. Our luggage was always an entanglement of trunks and boxes and pictures wrapped in blankets. Also the cats' tray filled with special cat litter so that I could let them out in the train. More often than not the porter would grow so confused that he would spill the litter beneath the train. I let the cats out of their basket when we were in the sleeper and Kit would try to catch the light reflected on the shiny objects with her paw as the train gathered speed into the night. They were a beautiful and strange pair, my beloved little cats.

*   *   *

I had to go to a funeral. An old lady who had once worked at Innisaonar had died. The funeral was to be held in the Episcopalian Church in Dornoch. In the Church of Scotland women never attend the actual burial of the dead but the old lady being English, I felt that I should go. I told Martin not to come as he had never met her. It was a simple service and the arrangements were carried out by Mr. Cameron, the chemist in Dornoch, who was much involved in the church. I was not deeply moved because the old lady had lost her memory and perhaps the time had come for her to die. A few cars drove behind the hearse to the cemetery which stands in a lonely plot of land. As I walked to the gate I was handed a piece of paper with a number on it. To my horror it meant that I was to be one of the pall-bearers. The chemist had thought that Martin would have attended the funeral. With Mr. Cameron the chemist, Dr. MacKenzie and several other men we carried the coffin to the grave. I remember the rope lowering the coffin, cutting into my hands as we slowly let it down. I remember the feeling of being so near to the outer side of death but still strangely distant.

As we walked away from the grave Dr. MacKenzie shook hands with a look of bewilderment on his old face.

*   *   *

It is strange how little I recall about the Barstows' visit. They were an American couple, friends of Martin's. Their son Joe came with them. I made their room as perfect as I could before they arrived. I put a small bouquet of roses beside their bed. White and pink roses packed tightly together, their petals just unfurling. The sun shone into the room and the flowers of the deep purple buddleia came in through the window. A red admiral butterfly fluttered against the pane.

There was tension between the three guests although we walked and laughed on a calm sunny day with the smell of wild thyme in the sand dunes.

Joe is now in prison. What lies in between those years?

*   *   *

Cape Wrath is a day's driving from Skelbo. Guy came in his Amphicar to stay with us. His Amphicar took to the water as well as to the road. We drove to Durness to reach the most western point of the British mainland. On expeditions to the interior we took flasks of hot soup and coffee, chickens and ham, salads and ginger beer. This day we ate our picnic beside the Kyle of Durness which can only be crossed by a ferry-boat. We ran the Amphicar into the water. Waves broke over the windscreen, the car rocking in the icy water. The kyle is not wide but it is rough as it flows in from the sea. The car heaved up on the other side on to the landing stage and we drove along the bare flat moor where wolves once lived. There is a lighthouse at Cape Wrath; as clean and shining as a naval ship; the white paint without a scratch and the brasses inside burnished. The wind at Cape Wrath prevents one going too near to the edge of the huge cliff. But it is possible to see hundreds of feet down; the water churning and hurling itself against the rock. A green and white mass of water seems to be endlessly in anger and in torment.

Guy caused much amusement with his Amphicar. He took Mrs. Murray for a ride on Loch Fleit, and a staunch and sporting land-owning lady with a large frame, across Little Ferry.

There are many matriarchs in Sutherland who, with their sporting life, remind me of the Valkyries.

Over the years at Skelbo we made many expeditions. One morning at breakfast when Maria and Richard were there, I said: 'Let's go to the Orkneys today.' Both Maria and I are afraid of flying and to reach the Orkneys for the day it is necessary to go by air. But during those happy times at Skelbo I had the *joie de vivre* of youth which I did not possess in London. We drove to Wick through the flat county of Caithness which is bare of trees and where the scarcity of the crofts immediately strike one. The sky meets the land, almost obliterating any horizon and it gives me a sense of desolate freedom. The churchyards have gravestones which are huge monuments with the trade or the occupation of the dead inscribed on them.

We flew from Wick airport in a small aeroplane, looking down at the green water of the Pentland Firth. Kirkwall, the capital city of the Orkneys has an atmosphere of its own. It is in a different country. It was wet and windy and St. Magnus, the rose-red cathedral, was closed. We tried every door and asked if we could enter but the Norse-blooded people would not allow us. Away from the small town of Kirkwall there is a feeling of depression and decay. The Churchill barriers still stand and everywhere are scattered old tin huts and objects of rusty iron which are relics from the war.

Another summer we drove to Applecross which lies in Wester Ross. It is a very long way from Skelbo. To drive up the steep, winding pass which is almost perpendicular reminded me of a fertile route in Northern Greece. But here there is no green, only barren land, and when the top of the pass is reached, a shining mass of pink rock, glistening in the sun. Applecross itself is green with sea-washed turf and the village prosperous-looking. We looked over to the Isle of Raasay which lies in the Sound darkly.

TO THE PLACE OF SHELLS

There were so many expeditions that we made. Along
the north coast of Sutherland to the cave of Smoo which
was one of Sir Walter Scott's favourite places; Loch
Eriboll, Betty Hill and to the House of Tongue. The west
coast with Laxford Bridge and Scourie; the huge rock
hills like Arkle, and the tiny hills of green and gneiss
which my father said reminded him of Palestine. In the
autumn the stags would be roaring. And then there is
Kinlochbervie; the Isle of Handa where in June, puffins,
guillemots and razor-bills nest in thousands on the rocky
ledges; that gaunt country where lochans shine like
mirrors amongst the hills. But I was always glad to get
back to Skelbo with its gentleness, with its farm and the
loch and the sea, and where I could breathe freely its
familiar air.

*　　*　　*

The absence of a child in my life became so acute that
Martin and I adopted Larissa when she was ten days old.
She arrived one morning in London in a large black car.
She lay in a basket which I had especially prepared for
her. A wool bonnet was pulled down over her nose
and she looked a small ugly thing. When I held her
for the first time I felt excited that she was ours, but I
had no real love for her. I prayed that we would grow
to love her and that I would still have a child of our
own.

We took Larissa to Skelbo with the cats when she was
two months old. She was very dark and she already had a
strong personality. We also took Miss Mason, a patient
and elderly person who was to look after her. I knew that
I should care for Larissa myself but Martin would never
have stood for the full-time relationship that a mother

153

and child should have. I made a nursery for Larissa at Skelbo, the walls covered in a paper of yellow roses. Over how many years had I longed to make a nursery, and to the outside world I was happy. Every day during the summer when the days were full of sun, Larissa lay in her pram with a canopy over it. I would place a rose beside her on her pillow; a red rose called Paul Neyron which was almost as large as her head. In the evening at ten o'clock I felt it my duty to go to her nursery while she had her feed. My visible happiness was not an inward one. I could not understand why this depression overcame me. We had a child in the house; something I had always craved for but yet what was lacking? Martin and I watched her grow with this visible happiness but was not the imprisonment of ourselves already starting?

Miss Mason – a delicate little woman who imme-diately became dedicated to Larissa – never once com-plained of anything. The only thing that puzzled her about Skelbo was that as she walked from the nursery to her own room she felt and saw a dark object following her. She said that it was not a cat or a dog but it was definitely the shape of some small thing. I never mentioned to her that the child of the tenant farmer who had been burned to death so long ago had slept in Larissa's nursery. I have already said that I never see such things, but for people who can, Skelbo is haunted. By those who wish one well. By the child who wants to join in.

During the days of November when Martin was away, Miss Mason, Larissa and I would go for long walks together. We put the pram in the back of the car and drove to different places. We would push the black pram up the little road to Thorbol Street. We pushed up the steep hill with the rocks and heather surrounding us. At the top there is a row of crofts where hens and ducks and geese are kept and where the sloping fields still have their

corn in stooks. A bitter wind blew and it started to snow
and we took shelter in the sheep and cattle byre with the
smell of hay and of the animals and of the warmth it
gave us. The rough shed protected the small baby in her
pristine white array. I felt safe there and wished to stay.
I heard the cow bells tinkling in the alder wood below
us. We walked on up past Thorbol Falls and the rowan
trees loaded with their scarlet berries. We walked along
this deserted road with the smell of the wet pink and
green sphagnum moss in the air, the dying bracken around
us and the peculiar feeling of melancholy which comes
at the back-end of the year.

The time came for us to go. I always hated leaving
Skelbo and every time I feared that I might never see it
again. There was the usual ordeal of the journey. Martin
could no longer stand the upheaval so he now always
went by car, starting in the middle of the night and
driving the six hundred miles to London without a break.
James Fraser was to drive us to Inverness. Martin handed
me the tickets before he left and told me the hour of the
train. It began to snow. We reached the station in good
time and I thought it strange that the entrance was locked.
I went to inquire and I was told that the train had left
twenty minutes before. There was no other to London
until the next night. I decided to try to catch the train
at its first stop which is Aviemore. The hotel porter looked
doubtful but I had a baby and two cats to think of, a
worried Miss Mason and a gardener not knowing where
he was going. I told James Fraser to drive as fast as he
could along the icy roads. We skidded several times and
Miss Mason clutched Larissa in her cot. The cats started
their howling and their cries became hoarser and hoarser.
When we reached the hills around Daviot a blizzard
began. In the darkness we could not see the road. I knew
that we were in danger. We had less than twenty minutes

to reach Aviemore. When we got to Tomatin I jumped out of the car near to a telephone box. I telephoned the station-master to ask him if he could hold the train for five minutes. He said he was sorry but it had already been delayed. I then knew that we were beaten. We searched for somewhere to stay the night and found rooms in a small hotel in Aviemore called The Cairngorm. My room had a large mahogany wardrobe standing in the corner. I let the cats out from their basket and immediately they jumped from the bed to the top of the wardrobe. They stayed there all night swishing their fluffed-out tails and growling and spitting. I sent James Fraser to his room and gave poor Miss Mason a glass of wine. She accepted it gladly. Never once did she complain.

There was a local train to Edinburgh early the next morning. The blizzard was still blowing and we sat huddled in the waiting-room on the deserted platform in the icy cold, the cats still howling and Larissa crying. At last the train came in; it was unheated and stopped at every station. Then we changed into the main train to the south. We had a long day's journey ahead of us. We sat and sat for hours on end. Even the cats were so tired that they gave up their cry. The blizzard continued until we reached the border country. Almost as the last snow-flake fell Miss Mason leaned forward and with her stoical pinched face brightening asked me: 'Are we in England yet?' That was the only moment when I could have hit her, so reluctant to leave Skelbo I had become. 'I have no idea where the border lies,' I answered her crossly. It would be difficult to forget that endless journey. We took it in turns to hold Larissa while she cried; the rest of the time she lay asleep in her basket cot. The cold and the lack of food made us speechless. The cat-litter in its tray mixed with baby paraphernalia, the luggage and Miss Mason and me; and our charges: Larissa and Kit and Tom. We reached London late in the evening and were met by Martin, he smiling and serene.

Shortly afterwards Miss Mason fell very ill and was forced to return to her home in the country, never to return. I wept.

*   *   *

The little River Carneigh has held a large place in our lives at Innisaonar and Skelbo. I still have the right to fish, but I rarely go. I no longer enjoy killing things.

But there was a day I went fishing with my father at the top end of the river by the Willow Pool. It was not one of the grey days when the country resembles a plain woman. All was brilliantly clear and shining. Our feet crunched on the pebbles by the river bank. I cast my fly into the deep pool with its fast running water where a bank of reeds jutted out. I had come to know that this was a place where fish often lie. Immediately I rose a fish and my father watched me playing it while the salmon fought for its life. Down the river and up again reeling it in, my rod bent as far as it would go. My father gave me instructions in a quiet voice on the bank. The fish leapt in the water. It was big for the River Carneigh. It fought for about twenty minutes, my strength waning as the fish's must have been. Eventually I managed to haul it on to the pebbles and my father killed it: a silver fish from the sea weighing ten pounds. I do not believe that my father liked killing fish. We clutched at each other and I felt as near to him as I had ever been. That rare closeness to my father which came so seldom. It was like a vivid blue streak in my life. And it was three weeks later that he died.

The last fish I killed in the Carneigh was against the

law. It was on a cold wet day in the autumn; Martin and I went with Alexander, a young neighbour, to the salmon-ladder. I held Larissa in my arms. The bottom pool of the ladder was swarming with fish. Every few minutes a salmon would leap, perhaps fall back again into the pool of the falls below and then try again successfully. The temptation was too much. I handed Larissa to Alexander and ran for my gaff which lay covered in the back of the car. Quickly I gaffed a fish and killed it and wrapped it up in a rug. We did not look like poachers. We stood so innocently by the pool with a baby in arms looking on.

On our return to Skelbo we learned that a famous actress was taking part in a film which was being made at Little Ferry. I do not know why they chose that place, so remote and unknown as it is. Martin and Alexander went to look at the scene while I cleaned my fish. They returned laughing, saying that the men were dressed as false Scots, as caricatures in tweed plus-fours and kilts and with a few sad-looking setter dogs hanging around. Martin had invited the actress to tea and she would be coming soon in her chauffeur-driven car. She arrived shivering with cold and drank two large whiskies. We sat in the panelled room trying to warm her by the fire. Somehow the news of the presence of an actress had gone quickly round the farm. Suddenly the little doors of the room were flung open. Mrs. Murray's son stood in the entrance. He planted his feet in the fourth position of a ballet dancer and his maroon-coloured beret was set firmly on his head. In a loud voice he cried: 'Mistress Ferguson,' and he gazed in wonderment at the bedraggled actress. She looked at him as though she were in a dream, not knowing where she had landed herself. She left shortly afterwards with her chauffeur for Inverness, to catch the train and get away from this strange place.

*　　*　　*

There were the days when we walked on the hill. In the late spring the sun-dew plant can be found growing in some boggy place. Also the pure wintergreen in the moss in the birch woods. We walked for miles and miles on the hill and occasionally a golden plover would whistle in front of us. Often I was afraid to be alone amongst the empty spaces where as soon as one horizon is reached another is revealed. We walked up the Strath Tollie burn which leads to Lochan Iain Buidhe which means Yellow John's Loch. It was here when my father was alive that we went once a year to collect the eggs of the black-headed gulls who nest there in a marsh.

Martin and I talked endlessly on our walks of enlarging Skelbo. Larissa was growing and our friends had more and more children. Martin was against the idea but I was determined to make Skelbo into a proper family home with larger rooms. We would return to Skelbo after our walks and at the bottom of the hill by the humped stone bridge which crosses the burn we would look up at the house and say: 'I wonder who lives there?'

Our plans for making Skelbo into a bigger house progressed. Richard, our friend, who was also an architect, was to design the new building. During the winter he drew plans. He and Martin had many arguments. The new building was to be in the same pink sandstone as the old part, adding another gable and with grey-green slates for the roof. The dining-room and the pantry and the kitchen were to be knocked into one, making a large drawing-room. A new dining-room and kitchen were to be built and a new nursery with three more bedrooms. There was to be a new hall and front door with flagstone steps leading up to it. The character of the house was to remain the same, with crow-stepped gables. It was a big undertaking but I had this dream which followed me wherever I went. Martin was restless that winter and instead of our lives drawing closer we became further and further apart. He seemed frustrated that I could not keep pace with his activities. I did not realize that I was leading an interior life where the visible world was diminishing day by day. I performed my duties for Larissa and did all that I should, but in the outer world my confidence was waning. At that time I had little to fulfil my inner life except for Skelbo where I watched and tended my plants and trees and watered my soul.

*   *   *

Larissa was christened when she was fourteen months old in the Episcopalian church in Dornoch. There was no font so she was baptised out of a shell. She wore a white muslin dress and with a lace patterned shawl made by Mrs. MacAlastair around her shoulders. Her feet were bare. We gave her the name Larissa because of her Slav blood, and also Marie, because I felt that she might have need of a Saint's name. The harmonium in the church gave out a hymn which sounded a little like a dirge. Afterwards there was a lunch for Larissa's godparents and the chemist who did so much work for the church. Mrs. Murray and Mrs. MacAlastair were also there. There was smoked turkey to eat and salads and special flageolet beans which Martin had bought for the occasion from Soho. Larissa sat in a fragile chair surrounded by her gifts and bottles of champagne. I see the young clergyman dressed in black in the little grey-green panelled room with a vase of white flowers behind him.

Shortly after, Martin and I went to a neighbour's wedding in the Scottish church in the small town of Golspie. In his address the minister spoke about how a marriage must be built like a house on rock and of how it should grow slowly to maturity. I felt the tears running down my face, because with us it was not so. Why did I feel that, when to the visible world all was well with Martin and me?

The work at Skelbo had already begun and the masons were carving and hacking their stone.

*   *   *

It was Larissa's first Christmas at Skelbo. As I held her on my knee she gazed in wonderment at the candle-lit Christmas tree as all small children do. That year we did not have a children's party. I felt that I could no longer manage it.

The work of building the house was to continue and everything had to be stored in the attic. We had been invited to stay at Craigeilisy House in Aberdeenshire for the New Year and it was our last night at Skelbo. That evening I worked and worked, packing things away. Even the cream-coloured velvet curtains in the panelled room had to be stored. Martin helped me and then suddenly got angry; he went into a rage because I would not bundle the curtains up and leave them in the attic to crease and get eaten by moths. They were extremely heavy and each curtain had to be taken down and carried and laid smoothly in a pile. I worked far into the night until everything was completed.

We drove away from Skelbo for Craigeilisy, knowing that when we returned the house would have taken on a new face, larger and undecorated with not enough furniture to fill the empty rooms. My dream was turning into reality but without the mature love which that minister had spoken of.

There were forty or more people staying in the castle of

Craigeilisy. Few knew each other and one wandered endlessly along the passages and into the rooms amongst the
different groups, sitting and eating and saying a word or
two. In spite of its size we found there was no room for
Larissa, so she and Molly, who was looking after her,
stayed in a small cold inn at the bottom of the drive,
Larissa in her white coat and bonnet. I worried for
them.

There was to be a dance held in the long hall on New
Year's Eve. Huge joints of meat and turkeys on silver
dishes were served for dinner. Every woman wore a long
flowing dress except for the housemaids who were to join
in the dance – men in kilts with pipers and a Scottish
reel band. There was champagne and every kind of drink
in abundance. I could not talk to the strange people. I
could not communicate. At the dance I stood looking at
the family portraits which lined the walls. I stood looking
at the gay dancers, longing to be able to join in. The
housemaids danced with one another and the man-
servants and the guests. I searched for Martin for pro-
tection and security but he was talking to one of the maids
and he turned his back on me. I felt strangely alone as
the New Year came in and one of the guests came up to
me and said: 'You look like a ghost.' At half-past three
in the morning I asked Martin if he would take me to our
room. There were so many passages and winding stairs
in the turret where we slept that it would have been impossible to have found it alone. He did so, but with
mounting anger, and then returned to the party. I was
tired and filled with despair. A painting of two pale-faced
Victorian girls looked down at me from an oval-shaped
frame.

The following day we walked with friends down the
drive which was lined with trees, beaten by the salt wind
from the sea. We went to the small granite harbour of

Craigeilisy where grey waves were throwing themselves against the pier. An icy wind blew. I went to see Larissa and Molly who were shivering in the inn. They had been kept awake all night by shouting, drunken people. I told them to be ready in the evening for our departure. On our way back to the castle Martin and I quarrelled in front of the other people. Once again I was filled with despair.

Slowly the guests started to leave. When the time came for us to go, the car broke down. Someone tried to tow us but it was of no use. It had given up. We arranged with a chauffeur to put it in a garage and we hired a taxi to take us the long drive to Aberdeen to catch the London train. We collected Larissa and Molly from the inn and as they climbed into the taxi Larissa's toy wooden balls fell out of a bag and rolled in the dark down the hill towards the sea. They were irretrievable.

*   *   *

The winter progressed slowly in London. We seemed to go to more and more parties of which I was afraid. I was waiting to be at Skelbo again and to see the new building but I felt I had less and less strength about me.

We were to have some friends to stay who had four children and a whippet. I knew that the whippet would see my little brown cats as rabbits in the distance and that it would immediately kill them. I refused to have the dog and I searched for a kennel where it could be left. I did not know the family very well and I dreaded their visit. They would need entertaining. Miss Jefferson, who was looking after Larissa, was so fussy and nervous at the thought of going to Skelbo that she wore me down and I felt that I would break. My father-in-law fell gravely ill and with thankfulness I had to cancel the visitors. Maria and Richard with their three little daughters were due to arrive and Miss Jefferson's anxiety became so bad that I arranged for her and Larissa to wait in London until after they had left.

The first glimpse of Skelbo through the trees – that was what I had been waiting for. We stopped at the bottom of the hill and looked up at the house. For a few minutes all movement came to rest. The house was much longer and the new gable gave more proportion to the little tower. Before it had looked slightly truncated but now it flowed in a line, the windows bright and shining. I realized that out of the past and for the future something lasting had been composed. For me it had a mysterious beauty which I had not thought would be possible. Inside the new part was bare and some of the rooms had concrete floors and undecorated walls but most of the house was habitable. The workmen were still finishing the details. The new nursery had a polished wooden floor and by the window we placed our old fair-ground horse, brightly painted and with the words 'Lovey Boy' on its neck. Next door, in Larissa's bedroom, there was a white painted cot and a photograph of my father when he was a child dressed in a sailor suit. The bookshelves outside the nursery were filled with my childhood books and those of my father and mother. Maria's children played in the nursery and I knew that it was Larissa who should have been there first.

As soon as we arrived Martin made a telephone call, to whom I did not know, but it spoilt the excitement of the adventure. I felt an unaccountable fear inside me.

We went for picnics on the beach and Martin amused the children by covering them up to their necks in sand. My wedding-ring fell off and I was certain that I would never find it again. I searched and searched, trickling the sand through my fingers, and it was like a miracle to me that I came upon it. Then there was a picnic in a derelict croft where we had been invited by a neighbour. The children lit candles and marched up and down singing songs. We played the game 'Rescue' and I forgot all and hid and raced amongst the bracken, running as fast as I could. Martin joined in and it was a happy and a treasured day.

Richard had to return to his work in London and the same afternoon as his departure Martin said that he was leaving too. There was a party in London that he did not want to miss and he also had other things to do. The shock was so great that he had not told me before that it rocked my faith in him. I tried not to show my unhappiness because an acquaintance from the south had arrived unexpectedly for lunch. He was a large man in bright checked tweeds and he wanted me to take him fishing. I trembled at Martin's going but I drove the man to the River Fleit. I knew that he would catch nothing as the river was calm without a ripple on its surface. The sluggish river, with its reeds and green vegetation, was more like some African scene and it would not have been unexpected had a hippopotamus reared out of the water. The man talked the whole time and I wondered if he had sensed the tense atmosphere at lunch and the hopeless state that I was in.

Martin returned and the normal pattern of life continued. One day on our return from the beach at Dornoch, he stopped the car and went to make an inquiry at the Royal Golf Hotel. I was surprised and thankful that he was taking an interest in something and my spirits rose a little.

It was on the evening when I knew that Martin was returning to London for several days that we quarrelled so badly. The reason was a trivial one but I felt the house to be full of misery. Martin left in the middle of the night. He drove off into the darkness in a storming rage.

Several days later the postman brought some letters for Martin addressed to him at the Royal Golf Hotel – they had been forwarded to Skelbo. One of the envelopes had a German stamp. I could not understand why they had been sent to that address and my heart was full of heaviness. That afternoon Maria and I took the children for a walk up Dunrobin Glen. We walked past the mill and the black pond where the white ducks swim and over the bridges of the burn up to the waterfall where the moss drips from the rock and the sound of rushing water soothes the mind. But my mind could not be soothed and I felt nothing except this dragging weight of misery. I told Maria about the letters which lay on the shelf in the hall and I asked her whether I should open them. I knew that it would be wrong but I could not go on any further. Maria was hesitant but she half-agreed with me. On our return I ripped them open and read page after page written in a difficult hand. They were love letters. Everything went black and I left the letters in the hall and went to sit by the fire in the panelled room. I wept and wept, not caring if Mrs. MacAlastair could hear. I could not believe it was true. It was as though a murder had been committed. I telephoned Martin and told him I had read the letters. He was angry and told me to forward them to him. He gave me no reassurances and said that he would return for a day or two to explain. All confidence I had vanished. I left the letters in the hall for several days, not daring to look at or touch them. I just gazed sadly at the stained-glass panel of a shell which Martin had bought for the door of the new hall.

Martin came back the day before Maria and the children had to leave. A stony politeness reigned over the house during the day but at night I went into the room where Martin was sleeping and I clung on to the orange velvet curtains. I recognized everything and remembered all we had lived for, but Martin left it alone like something he had been concerned with long ago. I clung on to the curtains like someone drowning and howled like a dog.

At lunch the next day there were raspberries and cream to eat and tears started to roll down my face. Martin was going and I could not bear the thought of it, neither did I want to be left alone. They all went in the afternoon and I started to wait in vain for Martin to return. I feared to go to London and I now feared for Larissa to come to Skelbo. At that moment I could not have managed her and so she remained in London. I held on to Skelbo. I would stay. The same evening that Martin left I wrote down in my diary T. S. Eliot's poem:

> The moonflower opens to the moth,
> The mist crawls in from sea;
> A great white bird, a snowy owl,
> Slips from the alder tree.
>
> Whiter the flowers, Love, you hold,
> Than the white mist on the sea;
> Have you no brighter tropic flowers
> With scarlet life, for me?

I walked through the new empty rooms with the cats following me, not knowing what I was doing.

*   *   *

I had to put up a façade, a pretence, as though nothing had happened. I went to stay for a few nights with neighbours where it was a happy family home. I picked flowers in their garden and arranged them in their drawing-room. White sweetpeas and dahlias in front of family photographs in silver frames. They had friends staying and one of them asked about me: 'Who is that gay and laughing girl?' Then I returned to Skelbo and behaved to Mrs. MacAlastair as I have said, as though nothing had happened.

One day James Fraser asked if he could talk with me. I stood beside the little man on the terrace with the faded buddleia flowers behind us and he said: 'I think you should know that there is scandal. You are being talked about all round the farm.' My reply to him was curt but I was filled with horror at his words. I wanted so much to keep my sadness from them and behave as though everything was normal. It was my only hope to keep things going. And might not Martin return? I feared to be amongst these gossiping people with no one to protect me. Martin and I had several conversations on the telephone. They always ended hopelessly. Storms of tears overcame me as I drove to Dornoch to buy food and I frequently had to stop the car because I could no longer see the road. Mrs. MacAlastair came at night to sleep in the house and we spoke of everyday things. One evening she took me outside to see the northern lights. They shone dimly behind Ben Bhraggie, with their arctic strangeness.

Every day I worked in the garden planting daffodil bulbs. I became increasingly active in order to ease my pain. I disliked walking round the farm knowing that I was the centre for gossiping tongues. Winter was approaching. Once again I heard the geese fly south. The first snow shower fell. Kit spent the time on her rug in the kitchen beside the Aga cooker. She and Tom were a comfort. Neighbours came over to see me. 'You cannot stay here alone all the winter,' they said. But I was too afraid to go to London and I had nowhere to go if I did. I immersed myself in improving Skelbo and I arranged for gates and fences to be erected in order to keep the cattle out. I watched the sheep in the fields in the darkening days, in that peculiar light, when the sheep appear motionless and carved out of wood, like those of Samuel Palmer's. I functioned automatically. I did not realize then that I was on a downward slope. All I knew was that as long as I had Skelbo I could go on.

Mrs. Murray on the farm fell ill. She had been strong and fit for all her sixty years. She had played a large part in our life at Skelbo and also at Innisaonar. She had sat for evenings with me, quoting poems of Burns which in her Highland accent sounded like magic. Her mother had remembered Patrick Sellar, one of the organizers of the Clearances. Mrs. Murray had been ill for several months but refused to go to a doctor. When at last she went she was very brave. To go to a Glasgow hospital instead of Inverness meant that it must be something very serious. I went to see her before she left and she said good-bye as though I would never see her again. Old Donald Murray, her husband, went with her. He had not left Sutherland since he was a boy. Mrs. Murray's illness concerned everyone on the farm. Before she left for Glasgow she had told Mrs. MacAlastair exactly where her coffin was to lie in the cottage.

Mrs. Murray was making a good recovery when early one morning the police telephoned to say that she had died. The farm went into mourning. I went to visit Donald Murray on his return from Glasgow. I sat with him and his two sons. I sat with them in their dark front room. The men cried with the heartbreak and despair of children. Their life stake had gone and I did not see how such helpless people could manage on their own.

On the afternoon of Mrs. Murray's funeral I shook with fear before I went down to the cottages where the service was to take place. My step-brother William and his wife had rented a house on the other side of Little Ferry. William, who had known Mrs. Murray as a child and youth, was to come to the funeral. He came to collect me and together we walked down to the farm. It was a grey, cold day. The hearse and the wreaths of flowers and the coffin were in front of the cottages. The men stood bravely in a row. A large group had gathered, standing in the mud facing the cottage; Mrs. Murray had been well known and respected in the neighbourhood. The women sat inside peering out behind the closed window. I stood outside with the group with William by my side. He lightly touched my arm in case I fell in the slippery mud. Suddenly I saw a woman looking at us with fury in her eyes. Some of them did not remember William from so long ago and I knew with discomfort that they could be thinking: 'How dare she bring her fancy man to the funeral.' The minister uttered his prayers and then the cortège moved away from the farm to the cemetery, the women staying behind. William had been chosen by Donald Murray to be one of the pallbearers to represent our family. Not until this was realized was I beckoned inside. I stayed at the wake for as short a time as possible and then went to look for the car to go to join William and his wife. I had told James Fraser to take it to drive the men to the cemetery. He did not return until late. The day had been too much and I was left with an intolerable depression.

I knew that the end was coming. Winter had arrived. Pressures were building. I talked to Martin on the telephone but he wanted things to stay as they were. I had to return to London to face my problems there.

I was forced to abandon Skelbo. The Frasers had to go. The windows of the little railway cottage were boarded up. The cats were to be sent to a cat's home. I knew that all was lost; that my life had come to an abrupt halt.

But on my last day at Skelbo I stood in a snow storm down by the loch, and suddenly an overwhelming exaltation came over me. I could not ever remember feeling such joy. A stillness formed. I bore Skelbo in my heart and peace descended upon me. My mind went out to a certain rowan tree on the hill and I was at one with it.